BRIAN JOHNSTON

Our God Reigns! The Awesome Sovereignty of God

First published by Hayes Press 2020

Copyright © 2020 by Brian Johnston

All rights reserved. No part of this publication may be reproduced, stored or transmitted in any form or by any means, electronic, mechanical, photocopying, recording, scanning, or otherwise without written permission from the publisher. It is illegal to copy this book, post it to a website, or distribute it by any other means without permission.

Brian Johnston asserts the moral right to be identified as the author of this work.

Brian Johnston has no responsibility for the persistence or accuracy of URLs for external or third-party Internet Websites referred to in this publication and does not guarantee that any content on such Websites is, or will remain, accurate or appropriate.

Unless otherwise stated, all Bible references are taken from the NEW AMERICAN STANDARD BIBLE®, Copyright © 1960,1962,1963,1968,1971,1972,1973,1975,1977,1995 by The Lockman Foundation. Used by permission.

Bible references marked ESV are taken from the The Holy Bible, English Standard Version® (ESV®) Copyright © 2001 by Crossway, a publishing ministry of Good News Publishers. All rights reserved.

First edition

This book was professionally typeset on Reedsy.
Find out more at reedsy.com

Contents

Foreword		iv
1	HEAVEN'S WORSHIP OF THE SUPREME RULER	1
2	THE FLOOD, BABEL & GOD'S CHOICE OF ABRAHAM	7
3	GOD'S BUTTERFLY	13
4	GOD RAISES UP PHARAOH TO SHOWCASE HIS POWER	19
5	IT'S THE SOVEREIGN GOD WHO SETS THE LIMITS	25
6	WHEN GOD AWAKES	31
7	GOD'S STRANGE WORK OF JUDGEMENT	37
8	THE ANOINTING OF A PAGAN MESSIAH, CYRUS	43
9	UNSCRIPTED PREPARATIONS FOR THE FULLNESS OF THE TIME	49
10	THE DEATH OF CHRIST AS SOMETHING FORE-ORDAINED	55
11	THE SETTING ASIDE OF ISRAEL TO BRING IN GENTILES	61
12	MANAGING THE WORLD	67
13	FINAL WORD ON PRAYER	73
14	THE OPENING OF THE SCROLL	79
15	EPILOGUE	84
MORE BOOKS BY THE AUTHOR		88
ABOUT THE AUTHOR		92
ABOUT THE PUBLISHER		93

Foreword

Are we masters of our destiny?

The English poet, Henley, of the Victorian Era, was faced with losing his leg. He rejected that first medical opinion (which was in favour of amputation) and travelled to Edinburgh where the famed Joseph Lister, the pioneer of antiseptic surgery, proceeded to save his leg. This must have led Henley to feel that he hadn't allowed his circumstances to get the better of him, and so he wrote his poem 'Invictus' of which the fourth verse says:

> It matters not how strait the gate,
> How charged with punishments the scroll,
> I am the master of my fate:
> I am the captain of my soul.

If, as seems likely, the 'strait gate' and 'the scroll' (with its punishments or judgements) are allusions to destiny in biblical terms, he would appear to think he could overcome all that had been decreed for him. His sentiment of 'bloody, but unbowed' has appealed to many since: such as, Aung San (father of Suu Kyi); Nelson Mandela (in Robben Island prison); and Winston Churchill who in 1941, and with Great Britain at war, paraphrased the last two lines of the poem, stating "We are still masters of our fate. We still are captains of our souls." It seems as if Henley's poem fragment has become the great meme of much of society since

– in the sense of an idea that has caught on and transformed popular thinking.

Is it a case of 'whatever will be, will be?' Or can human destiny be shaped, even controlled – by humans? In the bigger picture, what governs history? Is it simply all left to chance? Some Greeks such as Democritus thought so, seeing nothing beyond materialism ('atoms and the void'). Other Greeks, such as Socrates, considered there was more – some form of transcendence. The writings of Homer and Hesiod talk about the Fates, the three daughters of the goddess of the night, Nyx. One of the Fates would spin thread from a spindle. The second sister would measure out a given piece of thread, signifying the length of a life. And the third sister would cut the thread, and that signified death. They were held to govern all events of human history and all events of a single life.

Doom-sayers who talk of the approaching 'end of the world' are met with patronising smiles worn by those who write about what they consider as the most serious global threats (choose from 'human extinction', 'global catastrophic risks', and eco-apocalypse) and proceed to offer strategies to protect the future of 'humanity'. They, too, believe they have strategies with which to master our destiny.

Society's meme or the Bible's theme?

Before writing this book, my daily Bible readings had been in the book of the Old Testament prophet, Isaiah. Between chapters 37 and 47, is found impressive testimony to the sovereignty of God. Some statements repeat again and again such as: **'Who is like God?'; 'Besides Him, there is no God'; 'He is the Lord, there is no other.'**

These statements, probably as much as any, ought to convince us that we must agree with God being sovereign, even if we don't understand always how that works. We actually rely on the sovereignty of God to make prayer effective and to guarantee the success of evangelism. Only atheists can seriously claim not to believe in the sovereignty of God. Because if God isn't sovereign, then he's not God. If there's anything outside of God's control – as someone as put it: 'if there's so much as one maverick molecule' - then there can be no absolute guarantee of anything. That works on the principle of the 14th century proverb: 'For want of a nail, the shoe was lost; for want of a shoe, the horse was lost etc. Even things that are not approved by God have been chosen by him such that they are permitted to occur. Nothing outside of God influences him because he is immutable - there is no change with God.

God's sovereignty is much more all-embracing therefore than the fact - although glorious - that Christ's death was effective for all those for whom it was intended to be effective (John 17:9 etc). These receive mercy; while all others receive justice. (There being no injustice with God).

The content of the chapters I've enjoyed seem to give distinguishing marks of God's sovereignty:

1. Nothing happens without God having done it. For example, the arrogant Assyrian oppressors are told they're only God's instrument (37:26). If there's calamity (or prosperity), then God caused it (45:7, not necessarily as a judgement but he chose not to prevent it).

2. God is the creator and sustainer of the universe. He stretches out the heavens like a curtain (40:22, no surprise then that there are indications that the universe is expanding). Human affairs as well as natural processes are all governed by him, who reduces rulers to nothing (40:23, a grain of sand in the kidney of Oliver Cromwell is said to have changed the course of western civilization).

3. God declares things to come and performs all his purposes (46:10). As Israel's God, he confronts the gods of the nations in a virtual courtroom battle, calling on them to *present their case* and their *strong arguments* (41:21-24). From the north and east, he was bringing a deliverer for Zion, announcing this before Judah even when into captivity (41:25-26). On the other side of the court, all his opponents and would-be rivals are impotent.

4. God avenges wrongs and restores justice (at times in strange ways, 28:21). As shocking as it was for Habakkuk to learn that the Babylonians would be God's instrument to judge; imagine the horror (captured in 45:9) when Isaiah announces a pagan messiah in the shape of Cyrus (45:1)!

5. God is the only saviour with whom forgiveness is found for his own names' sake (45:22). The historical setting for God's announcement of his superiority over all challengers is quite extraordinary. He's the all-powerful God of a downtrodden nation; whereas the then world superpowers were championing their impotent deities. Apparent success can be deceptive. Where was God at Calvary (and at 9/11, and now ...)? The answer is: 'On the throne.'

6. God will brook no rival nor give his glory to another - there is no other. In what seems like a parody, Babylon announces 'I am, and there is no one besides me' (47:8,10). The nations carry the images of their gods; but God carries his people (46:1-4). The profound reality is God has no equal.

So, it's not 'what governs history?' But it's 'who governs history?' God's sovereign providence governs all things.

One of the old Princetonian scholars, Archibald Alexander, put it like this: he said Christians ought not even to retain and use the word *fate* because it's so inconsistent with the truth. He went on to reference Nehemiah 9:6: "You, even you, are Lord alone. You've made heaven and the heavens of heavens and all their hosts. You've made the earth and all things that are in it and the sea and all that is in it. You preserve them all." He then draws attention to such passages as Luke 12:7, Matthew 10:29, Matthew 6:28, and Psalm 147:9. Put all that biblical material together, and what do you find? Even the hairs of our heads are said to be numbered. The birds of the air, the lilies of the field, and even the smallest creatures are all under God's care.

That's what led to the writing of this book: the clash between a cultural meme ('we are masters of our own destiny') and the Bible's theme ('none can stay God's hand – or resist his will'). In picking its way through this subject, there are a few key questions that the book raises and seeks to answer. Here are just some that may attract attention:

- Why bother praying?
- Why did God order the killing of peoples in the Old Testament?
- Has Israel been left out of God's purposes?
- Does God change his mind?
- What are God's purposes in the end times?
- Was Jesus' crucifixion simply a terrible accident?
- Are the 'sign gifts' part of God's plan for today?
- Does God decide who is saved and who isn't?
- What does the Bible categorically say about human origins?
- Do we have freewill?

Any worldview must answer four questions: concerning our origins, our morality, our (life's) meaning, and our destiny. The Biblical worldview does that by declaring – and demonstrating – God's sovereignty over all things. This book is offered in the hope that it may help the reader to discern which among the suggested answers we encounter today owe more to our culture's meme than the Bible's theme.

1

HEAVEN'S WORSHIP OF THE SUPREME RULER

Heaven's worship of the supreme ruler seated on the throne is captured in these verses:

"... they do not cease to say, 'HOLY, HOLY, HOLY is THE LORD GOD, THE ALMIGHTY, WHO WAS AND WHO IS AND WHO IS TO COME.' And when the living creatures give glory and honor and thanks to Him who sits on the throne, to Him who lives forever and ever, the twenty-four elders will fall down before Him who sits on the throne, and will worship Him who lives forever and ever, and will cast their crowns before the throne, saying, 'Worthy are You, our Lord and our God, to receive glory and honor and power; for You created all things, and because of Your will they existed, and were created'" (Revelation 4:8-12).

God's name is closely related to the verb 'to be' – as in the great I AM. Here in verse 8 he is described as the one who was, and is, and ever will be. And the angelic beings address God as 'holy, holy, holy.' The primary meaning of 'holy' is God's 'otherness' (before it affirms the thought of his moral purity). The fundamental difference between God and us is exposed here in the worship of heaven. God's holiness, that is, his otherness, is presented in exactly these terms: he's singled out uniquely as the one who always had, has, and will have, being – whereas, by contrast, all created things we're told came into existence by a sovereign act of his divine will.

To borrow from historic Christian teachers, God is not only the supreme Being, but he is a necessary Being. What that is saying is this: God absolutely must be; he simply cannot NOT be! If God were to cease to be, the universe would vaporize and just disappear. Looking at it the other way round, this has been used as a classic argument for the existence of God. For, suppose God did not exist, and that there once truly was 'not anything' (not even a sea of energy obeying scientific laws) - then there still would be and could only be nothing now. There is no such thing as a 'free lunch.' You can't get something out of nothing. Not spontaneously; not in 20 billion years. To believe otherwise, is to believe in magic – in fact it's worse than that: it'd be like pulling a rabbit out of a hat – without the hat, and without the magician!

And that brings us to verse 11. It's God's unique prerogative to bring something out of nothing. Verse 11 says God created all things and because of his sovereign will they came into existence, into being. There is no other possible (logical or scientific) explanation. Let all enquiry stop and worship begin ... as it continues in heaven. To find more detail, let's turn to the other end of God's Word, the Bible – and to its first book, the book of Genesis. Let's revisit some basic things the Bible makes very plain.

1) First, creation was by the word of God and, in particular, by Christ.

Genesis 1 repeatedly has the phrase "And God said." The person whom the Bible reveals to us as Jesus Christ (Colossians 1:16; John 1:1-3) is later identified as the agent of creation. The Bible offers us many proofs that Jesus Christ is fully God and fully man. Nothing else satisfies all the facts. On earth, by merely speaking, the God-man, Jesus of Nazareth, performed wonders instantly in the natural world. His word alone was enough to heal the paralyzed and tormented; and to raise the dead (Matthew 8:8,13; John 11:43). And there was an immediate response to it, such that we read that the wind and the waves immediately obey the voice of Christ (Matthew 8:27).

Genesis, and the Bible as a whole, knows of no process being used in creation, only the word and will of God. This agrees fully with our opening words taken from the last book of the Bible, the book of Revelation: [God] created all things, and because of [his] will they existed, and were created. The scientific laws we can discover (by 'thinking God's thoughts after him,' as Kepler said) regulate how the completed universe continues to operate.

2) Second, let's check out what the Bible says about human origins.

A straightforward reading (but confirmed by experts) of the opening chapters of Genesis leaves no doubt that we're engaging with Hebrew narrative, and not Hebrew in its poetic form. The Bible's first book tells us plainly that Adam was not made from, nor did he come from, any pre-existing living creatures. Rather, it actually says that he was made (directly) from the dust. Genesis 2:7 says: *"And the LORD God formed* man of the dust of the ground, and breathed into his nostrils the breath of life; and man became a living soul."

In this way, man is made in the image of God and is different from the animals (Genesis 1:27; 1 Corinthians 11:7). Opinions and speculations abound, of course, but if we take the Bible at all seriously, surely we'd want to weigh the precise meaning of man being formed from the dust of the ground alongside Genesis 3:19 which states, *"Till you return to the ground, Because from it you were taken; For you are dust, And to dust you shall return."*

Our decay back to dust at death is not a poetic description but is sober reality. This leaves us with no choice over how to understand the Bible's meaning about human origins. Taken together, the texts in Genesis 2:7 and 3:19 plainly mean Adam was made from actual dust in the first place, and not from a pre-existing creature.

3) Third, mentioning death raises the question about its existence before the fall of man.

Six times God declared that what he'd made was 'good' in Genesis 1, before finally and emphatically signing everything off as 'very good' in verse 31. The living creatures (of Genesis 1:20,21 and 30) are spoken of as possessing life in the same sense as humans do (in Genesis 2:7) – that is, they're spoken of as living creatures or living souls. Not even the living creatures were to be killed for food at this (pre-Flood) stage (Genesis 1:30). There was no sense of a suffering world, or of a world groaning under a curse. It was Adam who introduced suffering and death to the pristine world of God's making (Romans 5:12; 8:20): *"... as through one man sin entered into the world, and death through sin, and so death spread to all men, because all sinned."*

The Bible will later, by the hand of the Apostle Paul (1 Corinthians 15:26), speak of death as an enemy. As such, it belongs to God's acts of judgement and not to his acts of creation. It might be wondered if this reference is restricted to human death (due to it being man who willingly disobeyed), but three chapters later Paul confirms the sub-human creation was equally affected, emphasizing this by adding that it was 'not willingly' affected (as opposed to the willing rebellion of the first human). The full text is: *"For the creation was subjected to futility, not willingly, but because of Him who subjected it, in hope ...* [and then adds] *... For we know that the whole creation groans and suffers ... until now"* (Romans 8:20,22).

But, for the sake of argument, let's assume that death was normal from the outset of creation among the 'lower orders' of God's creation, but that it simply stopped applying to humanity during the time of their 'innocence.' Then the entirety of God's creation could hardly have been described as 'very good' – unless 'nature red in tooth and claw' can somehow be thought of as consistent with 'very good.'

The meaning of all this is confirmed by the biblical principle of a life for a life (see Leviticus 17:11,14). Human life is forfeit because of sin, and forgiveness is explained as being through the sacrifice of the life of an animal substitute. Blood-shedding is the way in which the taking of life is described. The blood of an animal was never for human consumption. This was because God had reserved it for the ritual forgiveness of human sin. When we reflect on the solemnity of this, do we seriously think that 'nature red in tooth and claw' could have been God's way from the beginning? The New Testament repeats that the penalty for sin is death (Romans 6:23), consequently, a blood sacrifice is needed to atone for sin (Genesis 3:21; 4:4; Hebrews 9:22).

It was consistent with this that Jesus Christ died as an atoning sacrifice when he died for human sins. And that was specifically because death had been introduced subsequently into a fallen creation as the punishment for sin (Genesis 2:17; 1 Corinthians 15:3). The Gospel, and so, our salvation, is predicated upon the first man, Adam, bringing death into the world by sinning; and then the second man, Jesus Christ, taking our place (1 Corinthians 15:21,22,45) By the first man came death; by the second man came life.

4) Fourth, the Flood was global.

Its global nature is readily proven from Genesis 7:19 – *"All the high hills, that were under the whole heaven, were covered"* and Genesis 9:15,16 – *"The waters shall no more become a flood to destroy all flesh. And the bow shall be in the cloud ..."* The rainbow covenant cannot possibly be referring to a localised flood, otherwise the covenant would have been broken many times over as many people have experienced local floods in many places over the centuries. Just as the Second Coming of Christ to the earth will be known universally (Revelation 1:7), so the Flood was universal, concerning the whole world (Genesis 6–9; Luke 17:24–26; 2 Peter 3). The Lord Jesus and the Apostle Peter each draw that parallel between the Flood and Jesus' coming back to the earth.

Any plain reading of the text tells us there was a world-wide Flood burying land-based, air-breathing creatures, which means that this currently cursed and groaning world is not what God started with, but one that's scarred by our human rebellion in the original sin. Isaiah 40 majestically declares the sovereign God as the creator of the ends of the earth: *"Have you not understood from the foundations of the earth? It is [God] who ... stretches out the heavens like a curtain and spreads them out like a tent to dwell in"* (Isaiah 40:21-22).

2

THE FLOOD, BABEL & GOD'S CHOICE OF ABRAHAM

The Bible's description of the global flood at the time of Noah is introduced to us as follows:

"Then the LORD saw that the wickedness of man was great on the earth, and that every intent of the thoughts of his heart was only evil continually. The LORD was sorry that He had made man on the earth, and He was grieved in His heart. The LORD said, 'I will blot out man whom I have created from the face of the land, from man to animals to creeping things and to birds of the sky; for I am sorry that I have made them.' But Noah found favor in the eyes of the LORD" (Genesis 6:5-8).

Wait a minute. Did God just say that he was sorry? Does, or can, an unchanging God change his mind? In the Old Testament, humans are only recorded repenting half a dozen times (e.g. Judges 21:6,15; Job 42:6; Jeremiah 8:6; 31:19; Exodus 13:17). For example, Job says: *"I retract, and I **repent** in dust and ashes."* But, when translated as 'to repent' like this or 'to be sorry,' the word – as at the Genesis Flood - is usually used of God. But, surely, God has nothing to retract? Or even regret? The fact remains, however, that in more than 30 other similar uses, the same word ('nhm,' Strong's #H5162) refers to the repentance of God, always having to do with his judgement (108 times in total, when including the sense of 'to comfort').

Equivalent New Testament words meaning 'repent' or 'repentance' have God as their subject only twice - and negatively at that: *"THE LORD HAS SWORN AND WILL NOT CHANGE HIS MIND* [or not repent], *'YOU ARE A PRIEST FOREVER'"* (Hebrews 7:21). And also: *"The gifts and the calling of God are irrevocable* [or unrepented of]" (Romans 11:29). In the interests of communication, God, is at times and in some ways, described in human terms – which can be misleading of course, for there can never be an exact correspondence. And there seems to be another layer of confusion when we come to 1 Samuel 15, for there God is twice said to have repented or regretted something; and twice it is said that he would never do such a thing (that is, never repent nor change his mind – same word used). What's going on? Well, here are the Bible's words, spoken to King Saul:

*"'Strike Amalek and utterly destroy all that he has' ... So Saul defeated the Amalekites ... But Saul and the people spared Agag and the best of the sheep, the oxen, the fatlings, the lambs, and all that was good, and were not willing to destroy them utterly ... Then the word of the LORD came to Samuel, saying, 'I **regret** that I have made Saul king, for he has turned back from following Me and has not carried out My commands'"* (1 Samuel 15:3-11).

*"So Samuel said [to Saul], 'The LORD has torn the kingdom of Israel from you today and has given it to your neighbor, who is better than you. Also the Glory of Israel will not lie or **change His mind**; for He is not a man that He should **change His mind**.' ... Samuel did not see Saul again until the day of his death; for Samuel grieved over Saul. And the LORD **regretted** that He had made Saul king over Israel"* (1 Samuel 15:28-35).

God is twice said to have done this, and twice it is said that he would never do such a thing - that 'thing' being 'repentance.' How can we resolve this? The answer is: God does not repent as we humans may repent, but there's a sense in which he 'repents.' At the root of the word in question is the expressive idea of giving a sigh, with the implication of being sorry. However, it doesn't have to be a guilty, regretful sorry, as when we say 'Oh, I'm so sorry!' It can be the type of sorrow felt by a parent when disciplining their child. It's not that the parent is unsure of his or her own actions, but could have wished the child's actions had been different.

When humans repent, they have a personal sense of having fallen short; and they feel this possibly with intense emotion; and it brings about a change in their behaviour. Here again is the case of King Saul: *"Saul said to Samuel, 'I have sinned; I have indeed transgressed the command of the LORD ... please pardon my sin and return with me, that I may worship the LORD ... I have sinned; but please honor me now before the elders of my people and before Israel, and go back with me, that I may worship the LORD your God'"* (1 Samuel 15:24-30).

The extent of any real repentance by Saul here is in fact questionable as it seems more like a lame excuse, as if he was saying to Samuel why don't we let bygones be bygones? By contrast, when the same word is used with God, we find that it's in the sense of others having fallen short; and about this God sighs. He sighs, as it were, with intense emotion - and he may adjust the timing of his judgement. It was in this sense that we read earlier: *"The LORD saw that the wickedness of man was great on the earth, and that every intent of the thoughts of his heart was only evil continually. The LORD **was sorry** that He had made man on the earth, and He was grieved in His heart"* (Genesis 6:5,6). God was sorry – not for anything he'd done: but for what they'd done – and of course, God wasn't surprised by human wickedness as though he never expected it. It wasn't the case that in retrospect he'd rather have avoided its occurrence - not at all. In his sovereign foreknowledge, he knew beforehand; but still he expresses pain when it occurs. God sighs with sorrow; he feels pain when executing judgement. God was sorry - not for anything he'd done or wished he'd done otherwise, but for what they'd done.

In his sovereignty, God can – and does at times - choose to change the timing of any judgement that's due. Here's an example of that from the prophet Amos:

"The Lord GOD showed me ... He was forming a locust-swarm ... I said, 'Lord GOD, please pardon!' ... The LORD **changed His mind** about this. 'It shall not be,' said the LORD ... The Lord GOD was calling to contend with them by fire ... I said, 'Lord GOD, please stop!' ... The LORD **changed His mind** about this. 'This too shall not be,' said the Lord GOD ... The Lord was standing by a vertical wall with a plumb line in His hand. ... Then the Lord said, '... I will spare them no longer'" (Amos 7:1-8).

That was two stays of execution, as it were – but fundamentally God doesn't go back on his word, only modifying the timing of his actions in a sovereign expression of self-control. In the case of Saul, earlier (1 Samuel 15), God doesn't revoke his underlying decision to let Israel have a king; the change is purely a tactical change to a better king. God deals with us as a potter deals with the clay in his hand (Jeremiah 18:7-10). There may be some variation in tactics, but no alteration to the overall strategy. We're told to pray, but not that it can change God's mind. God is immutable, and cannot be influenced by anything that's not from himself.

Through Malachi (3:6) God says, "For I, the LORD, do not change; therefore *you, ... are not consumed."* Now, it certainly would be unfair if God didn't recognize times when humans do change through the intervention of God's own sovereign grace. Take the well-known case of Nineveh. Its doom didn't materialize in Jonah's day, but later the prophet Nahum wrote about it. God's attitude against sin is always the same; but his attitude to the sinner corresponds with how he himself has changed the sinner's attitude to sin. It's precisely that which shows his consistency!

Our research into this topic, you remember, started out from the way the Bible introduces God's decision to destroy the world with a flood. The words of Psalm 29:10 can be applied there: *"The LORD sat as King at the flood; Yes, the LORD sits as King forever."* But, for some people, that raises the charge: "If God is good, how could he wipe out all those people in the Flood?" Here, the questioner, usually an atheist, doesn't take the time to consider his or her own presuppositions. What basis do atheists have with which to question the character of God - given that they have no objective moral foundation on which to do so? Morality for an atheist is just a matter of opinion. God is the sovereign creator and therefore has the right to do what he pleases: *"Whatever the LORD pleases, He does, In heaven and in earth, in the seas and in all deeps"* (Psalm 135:6).

Not long after the Flood, we come to the scattering of the nations of earth at the Tower of Babel, another major and obvious sovereign intervention by God into human affairs. We read:

"Now the whole earth used the same language and the same words. It came about as they journeyed east, that they found a plain in the land of Shinar and settled there. They said to one another, ... 'Come, let us build for ourselves a city, and a tower whose top will reach into heaven, and let us make for ourselves a name, otherwise we will be scattered abroad over the face of the whole earth.' The LORD came down to see the city and the tower which the

sons of men had built. The LORD said, 'Behold, they are one people, and they all have the same language. And this is what they began to do, and now nothing which they purpose to do will be impossible for them. Come, let Us go down and there confuse their language, so that they will not understand one another's speech.' So the LORD scattered them abroad from there over the face of the whole earth; and they stopped building the city" (Genesis 11:1-8).

God stepped in because the nations of the world had shut him out of their plans. Now, in the next chapter of Genesis, God shuts out the nations from his plans, by beginning again with one man. It had been Adam, then it was Noah, now it's Abraham:

"Now the LORD said to Abram, "Go forth from your country, And from your relatives And from your father's house, To the land which I will show you; And I will make you a great nation, And I will bless you, And make your name great; And so you shall be a blessing; And I will bless those who bless you, And the one who curses you I will curse. And in you all the families of the earth will be blessed" (Genesis 12:1-3).

These are all times when the unchanging God radically changed the course of history.

3

GOD'S BUTTERFLY

> For want of a nail, a shoe was lost,
> For want of shoe, a horse was lost
> For want of a horse, a battle was lost
> For want of a battle, a kingdom was lost,
> And all for the want of a horseshoe nail.

That rhyme is said to be based on the defeat of England's King Richard III at the Battle of Bosworth Field in 1485. This was immortalized by Shakespeare's famous line: "A horse! A horse! My kingdom for a horse!" What happened? Well, Henry, Earl of Richmond, was marching against King Richard the Third. King Richard knew it would be the fight of his life, for Henry wanted the throne of England. This contest would determine who would rule. On the morning of the battle, Richard sent to make sure his horse was ready, but the blacksmith had run short of nails with which to shoe the horse, with the result that its shoes were not fastened as firmly as they might have been. In the battle, one of the horseshoes came off the horse, and it stumbled, as a result the king fell, and so was lost both the battle and the kingdom. The moral of the story is that large consequences can be traced back to small events.

In the message of Christianity, Jesus' death and resurrection is central. His death outside the city wall of Jerusalem was the result of him being rejected by his fellow-countrymen, the Jews. As the Bible records, he'd come to his own people, but they'd not been willing to receive him (John 1:12). This, after all, was a people with a track record of reacting badly to those whom God sent to them, also known as prophets. God had put up most patiently with this type of behaviour, right from the start of their relationship with him. They'd formally become God's chosen people very soon after God had delivered them from their slavery to the Egyptians. That predicament of finding themselves enslaved to others was the result of changing leadership over time in the land of Egypt – the land to which they'd initially been invited as guests and where they'd previously found a royal welcome.

Before that, it was a famine that had first turned their eyes towards Egypt. In Egypt there was food, but where they were living there was none. The more favourable circumstances prevailing in Egypt were due to some astute crisis management by a man with God-given insight. And curiously this man was not an Egyptian, but someone who'd first gained his reputation in that land while being held in prison there. He really ought never to have been in prison in the first place, because he'd been falsely accused of doing wrong while in reality doing what was right. But he was powerless to defend himself because of his employment status. This itself was the result of an extreme case of sibling rivalry, whereby his own brothers had sold him into slavery and he'd been traded in to Egypt as a teenager. And what had been the start of this domestic abuse? Nothing more – and nothing less – than his father showing favouritism towards him, and his brothers resenting it.

Long story short: those today who are Christians can trace the blessing of their forgiveness back through one man's unwise parenting skills! Of course, it can be traced much, much further back than that – something that's made known to us by the Bible's revelation going way back beyond history itself. Joseph, for of course, he was the Bible character at the receiving end of his brothers' jealousy, summed it up like this in a remarkably gracious speech to his brothers when he was reunited with them and forgave them. He said: *"As for you, you meant evil against me, but God meant it for good, to bring it about that many people should be kept alive, as they are today"* (Genesis 50:20).

We can detect not only grace, but deep understanding in Joseph's words. But perhaps he spoke even better than he could know. For we've traced the flow of events over a much longer period than he was able to. Joseph's brothers 'meant evil' - and no-one other than themselves was responsible for that. But God 'meant it for good.' God's controlling of all events does nothing to lessen the responsibility of the human characters involved in the unfolding drama of history. The Apostle Peter's preaching soon after Jesus had been crucified makes that clear:

"'AND IT SHALL BE THAT EVERYONE WHO CALLS ON THE NAME OF THE LORD WILL BE SAVED.' *Men of Israel, listen to these words: Jesus the Nazarene, a man attested to you by God with miracles and wonders and signs which God performed through Him in your midst, just as you yourselves know – this Man, delivered over by the predetermined plan and foreknowledge of God, you nailed to a cross by the hands of godless men and put Him to death. But God raised Him up again, putting an end to the agony of death, since it was impossible for Him to be held in its power ... when they heard this, they were pierced to the heart, and said to Peter and the rest of the apostles, 'Brethren, what shall we do?'"* (Acts 2:21-24, 37).

Once again, by the Spirit, Peter doesn't offer any reduced human responsibility on the part of those actively involved – even on account of the fact that God had pre-planned it; for he says in no uncertain terms "you nailed [him] to [the] cross." This had the effect of producing a true acknowledgement of their personal responsibility and guilt: "What shall we do?" God's not remote from our everyday lives: he's not at all disinterested in the here and now. There's quite a popular view that imagines God as the reason for setting everything going at the beginning, but which also believes that he's someone who retains no interest in the day-to-day affairs of his world. Nothing could be further from the truth. Nothing is too small to escape his notice.

There's a popular notion that's called the 'butterfly effect.' It's the phenomenon whereby a small local change in a complex system can have large effects elsewhere. The butterfly effect is the idea that when a butterfly moves its wings somewhere in the world it can cause a tornado in another part of the world. World War II didn't start with some massive machinations of world leaders. Rather, it culminated into a wide-scale butchery just because of a very small incident in June 1914. Franz Ferdinand, the crown prince of Hungary, was going on a ride in a street of Bosnia, when his driver mistakenly took a wrong turn, and by chance bumped into a revolutionary named Gavrilo Princip.

The revolutionary, seeing the opportunity, instantly shot Ferdinand and his wife, who both succumbed to their injuries. Their death led to declaration of war by Austria-Hungary (supported by Russia) on Serbia, and the frenzy was soon joined by countries like Germany, France, and Britain due to several diplomatic treaties signed during that time, which blew into a full-scale world war. From this came the Versailles' treaty that led to Germany's humiliation. This gave Hitler the opportunity to come to power, and this resulted in a further World War with six million

Jews and 60 million other lives lost. All from a driver's wrong turn in Bosnia.

One preacher commented: 'One maverick molecule running loose in this universe outside the sovereignty of God could be the very thing that disrupts every promise God has ever made to his people!' By that remark, he was underlining the sovereignty of God. Nothing – no single event, however small – is untouched by his sovereign rule. As the Bible prophet Amos said: *"If a calamity occurs in a city has not the LORD done it?"* (Amos 3:6). The Bible proverb proclaims: *"The lot is cast into the lap, but its every decision is from the LORD"* (Proverbs 16:33). The most seemingly fortuitous events are ordered by God. The 'casting of the lot' or, as we would say, 'the roll of the die,' is symbolic of the part that human effort plays in the government of the world - God is above and behind it, but he doesn't work without it.

A grain of sand in the kidney of Oliver Cromwell changed the course of western civilization. Let me explain. Oliver Cromwell was a political and military leader in 17th century England who twice led successful efforts to remove the British monarch from power. Cromwell died from kidney disease, or a urinary tract infection, in 1658 at age 59 while still serving as Lord Protector. His son Richard Cromwell assumed the post, but was forced to resign due to a lack of support within Parliament or the military. In the leadership vacuum that ensued, George Monck assumed control of the New Model Army and spearheaded the formation of a new Parliament, which proceeded to pass constitutional reforms that re-established the monarchy. (In 1660, Charles II, who had been living in exile, returned to England to assume the throne, thereby beginning the English Restoration.)

Cicero once apologized for Jupiter's neglect of earthly affairs. He stated that the sovereign of the universe was on the whole a good sovereign, but with so much business on his hands, he had no time to look into details. The Judeo-Christian God of the Bible is not like that: *"I am the LORD, and there is no other; Besides Me there is no God ... That there is no one besides Me. I am the LORD, and there is no other. The One forming light and creating darkness, causing well-being and creating calamity; I am the LORD who does all these"* (Isaiah 45:5,7).

4

GOD RAISES UP PHARAOH TO SHOWCASE HIS POWER

The escape of the Israelites out of Egypt is the main Bible example of deliverance – symbolising the deliverance God offers us in and through Jesus, his son. If we're at all familiar with the basic storyline of the Old Testament, then we can conjure up in our minds the stand-off between Moses and Pharaoh. This was so much more, as the Bible tells us, than the leader of the enslaved people pitting his wits and will against the leader of their oppressors – with both sides invoking their respective deities. At one point, God addresses Pharaoh: *"But, indeed, for this reason I have allowed you to remain, in order to show you My power and in order to proclaim My name through all the earth. Still you exalt yourself against My people by not letting them go"* (Exodus 9:16-17). That's how involved God was in this event.

But let's start further back in history, with a woman praying about her difficult pregnancy: *"The LORD said to her, 'Two nations are in your womb; And two peoples will be separated from your body; And one people shall be stronger than the other; And the older shall serve the younger'"* (Genesis 25:23).

I think we can assume that Rebekah, the woman in question, shared this revelation with her husband. Isaac, however, seemed partial to his eldest who was an outdoors action figure, a game hunter. He was definitely partial to the food Esau, his eldest, served him. On the other hand, Rebekah's favourite was Jacob. But even if this was because she remembered God's prediction, she didn't seem to believe God could keep his promise without her using her own cunning to give him some assistance. But we're running ahead - the children haven't even been born yet. Let's go attend the birth:

"When her days to be delivered were fulfilled, behold, there were twins in her womb. Now the first came forth red, all over like a hairy garment; and they named him Esau. Afterward his brother came forth with his hand holding on to Esau's heel, so his name was called Jacob; and Isaac was sixty years old when she gave birth to them" (Genesis 25:24-26).

It does seem that in his early life Jacob couldn't wait to get his hands on what was his brother's! God had told Rebekah the way things were going to be – with her older son serving his younger brother – and he'd said this not based on their respective performances in early years. He decreed this before they were even born, so obviously it was quite independent of anything they'd done; that didn't come into it. In fact, God specifically wants us to notice this. Let the apostle Paul explain it from Romans chapter 9 – he's talking about God's purposes with Israel:

"Rebekah also, when she had conceived twins by one man, our father Isaac; for though the twins were not yet born and had not done anything good or bad, so that God's purpose according to His choice would stand, not because of works but because of Him who calls, it was said to her, 'THE OLDER WILL SERVE THE YOUNGER'" (Romans 9:10-12).

And in case we should think this is an isolated case, as opposed to something illustrating a divine principle, Paul adds our earlier example of the Pharaoh at the time of the Exodus:

"What shall we say then? There is no injustice with God, is there? May it never be! For He says to Moses, 'I WILL HAVE MERCY ON WHOM I HAVE MERCY, AND I WILL HAVE COMPASSION ON WHOM I HAVE COMPASSION.' So then it does not depend on the man who wills or the man who runs, but on God who has mercy. For the Scripture says to Pharaoh, 'FOR THIS VERY PURPOSE I RAISED YOU UP, TO DEMONSTRATE MY POWER IN YOU, AND THAT MY NAME MIGHT BE PROCLAIMED THROUGHOUT THE WHOLE EARTH'" (Romans 9:14-16).

There's something profound here; we've been allowed some insight into the sovereign workings of God. In this latest Bible example of Pharaoh, king of Egypt, if we were to check back to the book of Exodus, and the story of how he refused to give the Israelites their freedom, we'd find that we sometimes read of Pharaoh hardening his own heart; and at other times, it's said to be God who's hardening his heart – which raises the potential conflict in our minds between divine sovereignty on the one hand and human responsibility on the other. How can we have a real choice if God has actually already chosen what's going to happen?

Perhaps we could try an analogy here. Even with our modern scientific understanding, in the natural realm there are other things we just can't seem to reconcile. Take the nature of light, for example. There's real evidence that light exists as light waves: some experiments show it to behave in a way comparable to say, water waves. But, at the same time, there's just as good evidence to show that light and its energy come in little packets, more like particles. The only way we can live with that state of affairs in the natural world is by inventing a name for it. An 'antinomy' describes the situation where we have two things which to us are contradictory, and yet there's good evidence for both. In a similar way the Bible most definitely teaches both divine sovereignty and human responsibility.

But we tend to shy away from things that are difficult for us to understand – like when it comes to God's involvement in making things happen - and so it's tempting to try to respond to this by saying, 'Oh well, God knows in advance what's going to happen, and so he can tell us in advance what the future holds. But that doesn't satisfy the language God uses here. Listen to this inspired commentary as Paul continues:

"So then He has mercy on whom He desires, and He hardens whom He desires. You will say to me then, 'Why does He still find fault? For who resists His will?' On the contrary, who are you, O man, who answers back to God? The thing molded will not say to the molder, 'Why did you make me like this,' will it? Or does not the potter have a right over the clay, to make from the same lump one vessel for honorable use and another for common use? What if God, although willing to demonstrate His wrath and to make His power known, endured with much patience vessels of wrath prepared for destruction? And He did so to make known the riches of His glory upon vessels of mercy, which He prepared beforehand for glory ..." (Romans 9:18-23).

In any case, when the Bible speaks of God knowing the future, the word means to know with approval – it's not a passive knowledge, nor can it be, where God is concerned. The question was asked there: "Who resists his will?" In terms of our salvation and eternal destiny, the Bible would fully support that no more than "God wills" to be saved will be saved; but equally, no fewer than the "whosoever wills" will be saved. In other words, no fewer than all who willingly come to Christ for salvation will be saved; but equally, no more than those whom the Father draws to his

GOD RAISES UP PHARAOH TO SHOWCASE HIS POWER

Son will be saved. It's not something based on any good in us as simply foreseen by God. God's sovereignty includes the fact that Christ's death was effective for all those for whom it was intended to be effective (John 17:9 etc.). These receive mercy, while all others receive justice (there being no injustice with God).

So the story of Pharaoh and the Exodus has plunged us into deep water, offering us a glimpse into something very profound. It all demonstrates God's sovereign grace. Really, Paul, by the Spirit of God, has anticipated in that passage we read from Romans chapter 9 all the questions we want to ask too! For example, if it comes down to the will of God operating in our lives, how come God can still find fault with us? Well, if we stay close to the language of the Bible - and in a subject like this we really have to - then we'd have to say that being of a depraved mind, and being dead in sins, we had no ability of our own to come to Christ for salvation, so it had to be God's work - but at the same time we were held responsible. After all, didn't Christ describe unbelieving Jews of his day as being like chicks that wouldn't come to the mother hen? He was holding them accountable, responsible for their response.

We then find an almost irresistible urge to cry out: 'But that's surely not fair!' (We have no ability, but God still holds us responsible!) And it's good that we feel like this, for again Paul by the Spirit anticipates exactly that kind of reaction – which reassures us that we must be on the right lines after all! And this is where Paul parks the debate: for it's ridiculous to think of the mere clay of humanity criticising the divine potter. But does that mean God is responsible for people going to a lost eternity? Not at all! There can be no injustice with God. All the clay was spoilt, but that wasn't the Potter's fault; and he certainly has the right over the clay to do with some spoilt part of it something which that part deserves no more than the rest.

Well, we can even thank Pharaoh for his contribution to helping us strip away any remaining pride we may still have in thinking we made even the tiniest contribution to our salvation. More importantly, this impressive teaching of God's sovereignty provides us with the last word in complete assurance that once saved, we can never be lost again. Let's not be foolish enough to expect we can fully get our heads round God and his perfect ways – but instead simply bow our hearts in worship!

5

IT'S THE SOVEREIGN GOD WHO SETS THE LIMITS

People wonder why God hasn't yet put an end to all the evil in the world. In the Book of Revelation (6:9 –11), the souls of those executed for their association with Jesus wonder why the sovereign Lord is taking so long to administer justice on those who executed them.

Genesis 15:16 begins to throw some light on this problem. God said he wouldn't allow Israelis to return to their homeland until the fourth generation. Does this delayed return clue us in on why God allows evil to continue with little restraint? The delay was for the reason that *"the sin of the Amorites has not yet reached its full measure."* Only then would God step in and deal with the Amorites. One writer (Derek Kidner, Genesis) says this is "one of the pivotal sayings of the Old Testament."

"God said to Abram, 'Know for certain that your descendants will be strangers in a land that is not theirs, where they will be enslaved and oppressed four hundred years. But I will also judge the nation whom they will serve, and afterward they will come out with many possessions. As for you, you shall

go to your fathers in peace; you will be buried at a good old age. Then in the fourth generation they will return here, for the iniquity of the Amorite is not yet complete.' On that day the LORD made a covenant with Abram, saying, 'To your descendants I have given this land, From the river of Egypt as far as the great river, the river Euphrates'" (Genesis 15:13-16,18).

Abraham would have many descendants. Those descendants would one day be taken captive and treated harshly. After four hundred years, Abraham's descendants would return to Canaan. Their return would coincide with God's judgment on the Amorites in Canaan. These prophecies were fulfilled when, after Joseph's death, Pharaoh enslaved the Israelites (who were living in Egypt at the time), until Moses brought the Israelites out of Egypt to the borders of Canaan. Joshua then led the people into Canaan and conquered the land. Joshua's conquest took place only after the sin of the Canaanites had *"reached its full measure"* (Genesis 15:16).

God has set many limits for humanity. For example, he's marked out man's appointed times in history and the boundaries of their lands (Acts 17:26). And Deuteronomy chapter 32 tells us not only about God's selection of Israel but also of their specific territory. God timed the arrival of his judgment with the fullness of the sin to be judged, not before. He was very longsuffering in actual fact. The God who's set an appointed day and judge for future judgment on the whole world, at that previous time in history, used the army of Israel as his appointed instrument of judgment on the Amorite peoples. But God says to Joshua, *"I brought you into the land of the Amorites ... and I gave them into your hand, and ... I destroyed them before you"* (Joshua 24:8). *God* did the destroying. It was by the hand of Israel, but it was the judgment of God.

As was the case in Abraham's day, we know that God's judgment is coming. Unlike Abraham, we don't have a timeline to give us an idea of when that day will be. All we know is that God's judgment has not yet fallen, God is patient, and perhaps the sin of these modern times 'is not yet full.' God's judgments always show his sovereignty. God reminds the Jews that they were naturally no more worthy of God's favour than the Canaanites, by telling them: *"Your father was an Amorite and your mother a Hittite"* (Ezra 16:3).

Who were the Amorites? They were descended from Emer, the fourth son of Canaan (Genesis 10:16). When we meet them in the Bible, they're living along the Jordan valley (Trans-Jordan, Numbers 13:29, 21:21-31; Joshua 5:1; Judges 11:13). The name Amorite is often used in the Bible for the Canaanites in general (Genesis 15:16; Amos 2:9); but the Amorite kingdom was a very ancient one. They gained control of most of the region of Mesopotamia from the Sumerians, maybe just after the time of Abraham. They re-established their capital in Akkad, changing its name to Babylon. The religion of the Old Babylonians perhaps stayed pretty much the same as it had been. The Amorites told stories of the king of the city-state of Uruk, an adventurer known as Gilgamesh, a rebel who defied the gods. Though the stories were Sumerian, the Amorites published them as part of their own literature.

The Amorites lived in close contact with the Sumerians for a long period of time before they took over from them. It's possible they adopted much of the Sumerian religion over time. They did merge a new god into the region's religion. Marduk came to assume the role of chief deity, and the story of his rise is known as the Enuma Elish. The Amorites also worshipped the moon-god, Sin. The Amorites dominated the history of Mesopotamia, Syria, and Palestine roughly between the times of Abraham and Moses. Tribal nomads, the Amorites were reputedly fierce warriors. Their most noted king, Hammurabi, was the first king of the Babylon Empire. He was best known for the set of laws called Hammurabi's Code, which forms one of the earliest surviving codes of law in recorded history. Later, the Amorites migrated or were pushed westward toward Canaan. Broadly speaking, the Amorite culture was Mesopotamian. The word for 'Amorite' comes from a Sumerian word ('MAR.TU') which vaguely referred to the area and population west of Sumer and Babylon.

God says through the prophet Amos: *"Yet it was I who destroyed the Amorite before them, whose height was like the height of the cedars ... Also it was I who brought you up out of the land of Egypt and led you forty years in the wilderness, to possess the land of the Amorite"* (Amos 2:9–10 ESV). The fact that at least some Amorites were unusually tall would have suggested that the native population of Canaan had an origin that recalls the events of Genesis 6:4, which describe relations between sons of God and daughters of men. When the 12 Israelite spies reported back to Moses what they'd seen in the land to be conquered, they described having seen giants, said to be derivative of the Nephilim (Numbers 13:32–33, see Genesis 6:4). A King Sihon was allied to a fellow named Og, another king of the Amorites who ruled in the region of Bashan. Og, too, was a giant.

Deuteronomy 3 (ESV) tells us what happened after Israel's battle with Sihon: *"Og the king of Bashan came out against us ... we devoted them to destruction ... So we took the land at that time out of the hand of the two kings of the Amorites who were beyond the Jordan, from the Valley of the Arnon to Mount Hermon ... Og the king of Bashan was left of the remnant of the Rephaim. Behold, his bed was a bed of iron. ... Nine cubits was its length, and four cubits its breadth, according to the common cubit"* (Deuteronomy 3:1–11 ESV).

Interestingly, these are precisely the dimensions of a cultic bed found by archaeologists in the remains of a ziggurat (Etemenanki). Og is said to have been the last of the Rephaim—a term connected to the giant Anakim and other giant clans in the Transjordan (Deuteronomy 2:11, 20). Apparently, the Rephaim are also mentioned by name in Amorite texts where they are described as dead warrior kings.

Israel's battles in the Transjordan begin to bring us face to face with an issue that's troubled Bible readers for centuries: the Amorite genocide. But more careful reading shows there was no indiscriminate and wholesale genocide - rather it appears it was specifically the bloodline of the giants (Genesis 6:4; Numbers 13:33; Deuteronomy 2:10-23; 3:1-13; Amos 2:9) that was *"utterly destroyed"* (e.g. Deuteronomy 3:6). Co-existence with them was intolerable. Quite distinct from that is the separate issue of the peoples to be dispossessed.

When we read *"so Joshua took the whole land ... had rest from war"* (Joshua 11:23), it suggests that success of the mission was defined early on mainly in terms of the targeted elimination of giant clans from the hill countries of Israel. The 'hill countries' refer to the central mountainous spine of Israel that's in 3 parts (Joshua 11:21). This defining event of the conquest is described in the Book of Joshua, chs.10-12. But there's a postscript: and it's the 'mop-up' operation led by Caleb that occurred afterward – and that also focused on the elimination of the giant clan of the Anakim - again in the hill country (Joshua 14 and 15). A last piece of mopping up in Philistia was left for David when he battled the giant Goliath (see 11:22).

And it's also made quite clear there was also no wholesale slaughter among the remainder. Aside from the Gibeonites (chapter 9); there was no dispossession of Maacathites and Geshurites (Joshua 13:13); Jebusites (Joshua 15:63); Canaanites at Gezer (Joshua 16:10); Canaanites at Megiddo, etc. (Joshua 17:12,13). This was not condemned later in

Joshua 21:43-45 where we read *"the LORD gave Israel all the land ... they possessed it ... the LORD gave them rest ... the LORD gave all their enemies into their hand."* That's a satisfactory report. In Joshua chapter 23 (vv.5,7,9,12 – and into the Book of Judges) it's made clear there was still at that late stage the potential to dispossess others, as well as a need to avoid intermingling and intermarriage with them (which presumes no wholesale genocide).

In short, the mandate for 'holy war' had awaited the time when 'the sin of the Amorite' had come to full measure or was complete (Genesis 15:16). The summary of the conquest given by Amos focused on the destruction of the giant clans: for we read that God *"destroyed the Amorite before them, though his height was like the height of cedars and he was strong as the oaks"* (Amos 2:9). In the Israelite conquest of Canaan, God was sovereign in its timing and extent.

6

WHEN GOD AWAKES

I'm reminded of the day recorded in the Bible when a young man was sent by his father on an errand to look for some lost donkeys. Totally unsuspecting, for little did he know he would be anointed as the first king of Israel before he returned home. The Bible Book of Proverbs says: *"You do not know what a day may bring"* (Proverbs 27:1). That was true of Saul that day.

In the historical psalm that is Psalm 78, the psalmist writes about God leading the Israelite people through the desert, guiding them like a flock. Often the people rebelled in the desert when they forgot the mighty works that had demonstrated God's power in the land of Egypt. Next up, the psalmist goes on to write about the conquest of the land (Psalm 78:55). That didn't turn out too well either:

"... God ... was filled with wrath and greatly abhorred Israel; so that He abandoned the dwelling place at Shiloh, the tent which He had pitched among men, and gave up His strength to captivity and His glory into the hand of the adversary. He also delivered His people to the sword, and was filled with wrath at His inheritance ... His priests fell by the sword ..." (Psalm

78:59-62,64).

God was angry and caused Shiloh to be plundered. The ark of the covenant was captured too (vv.59-61; cf. 1 Samuel 4:4-11). Many people were killed at that time (Psalm 78:62-64), including the priests Hophni and Phinehas. The battle of Aphek was a particularly low point, even by the standards of the very patchy history of God's Old Testament people. But then the same psalm, Psalm 78, tells us this happened:

"Then the Lord awoke as if from sleep, like a warrior overcome by wine. He drove His adversaries backward; he put on them an everlasting reproach. He also rejected the tent of Joseph, and did not choose the tribe of Ephraim, but chose the tribe of Judah, Mount Zion which He loved. And He built His sanctuary like the heights, like the earth which He has founded forever. He also chose David His servant and took him from the sheepfolds; from the care of the ewes with suckling lambs He brought him to shepherd Jacob His people, and Israel His inheritance. So he shepherded them according to the integrity of his heart, and guided them with his skillful hands" (Psalm 78:65-72).

Doesn't that just grab our attention? The writer describes the Lord's intervention as being, figuratively speaking, like a mighty man awakening after having been put to sleep by wine. He woke up, rose up, and saved his people from their enemies. But then he rejected the tents of Joseph, the tribe of Ephraim, representing the Northern tribes, and chose Zion – down south in Judah - for the location of his sanctuary. He also chose the shepherd boy, David, to be his king. Disbelief and disobedience by God's people, Israel, had led to their disastrous defeat at the Battle of Aphek (1 Samuel 4:1-11), but it was to mark the turning point of the way that would lead to a new sanctuary and a new king to lead the people.

In the picture language the Psalmist gives of God arousing himself, as a mighty man refreshed by sleep and wine, and shouting for the battle, there's poetic licence in the use of human language to describe God's actions. God never sleeps; his control of human affairs is continuous. **God's sovereign superintendence is at times hard to detect; at other times it's dramatic.** But his activity is constant. There are periods in which his hand can't be seen in human affairs – when he seems to be indifferent to the interests of his people, as though he was sleeping. However, at those times, the continuous operation of God's rule is simply not being appreciated by us. For a time, God appeared to resign his control of Israel's affairs and to surrender them to their enemies. Now that his hand is again visibly active, the poet pictures him as a mighty warrior arousing from slumber – refreshed by sleep and wine - and shouting with a desire to battle with his foes.

What did this awakening mean for Israel? In part at least, it was a spiritual awakening in the life of David. God deposed Ephraim from the priority that tribe had previously held. Instead, he *"selected Judah to become the location of his sanctuary."* Within its territory on Mount Zion, the sanctuary or temple was established, and the seat of government placed. And out of Judah, King David was chosen. He was the leader who finally and decisively captured Jerusalem after some previous false dawns during Israel's early history in their promised land. All this was in line with God's sovereign purposes. The supremacy of Judah had been predicted by Jacob long before (Genesis 49:8-10). From that tribe, the Messiah was to come.

Another psalm, Psalm 68, captures a sense of surprise at God's choice of Zion, a seemingly lesser mountain: *"A mountain of God is the mountain of Bashan; a mountain of many peaks is the mountain of Bashan. Why do you look with envy, O mountains with many peaks, at the mountain which God has desired for His abode? Surely the LORD will dwell there forever"* (Psalm

68:15-16).

Equally surprising was God's selection of David to be king. The psalm we read says: *"He also chose David His servant and took him from the sheepfolds."* Again, a remarkable example of divine sovereignty! God chooses a man of humble position to fill the most exalted position. David was even overlooked by his own father. It's as if he was a nobody at home, not given much esteem, only left with the job of caring for the sheep. He was bred not as a scholar, not as a soldier, but as a shepherd. He was chosen not for his appearance or position, but for his ability and character. This was the setting for God revealing something characteristic of his methods to Samuel, the prophet sent to anoint the teenage David: *"Man looks on the outward appearance, but the Lord looks on the heart."*

But as a shepherd, David had excelled. He was no hireling. He'd risked his own life to defend some members of his flock. He seems to have been particularly careful of *"the ewes with suckling lambs."* Having been faithful and gentle in his lowly sphere, God raised him to the honour and responsibility of the throne. Later, Jesus would use a parable to teach that those who prove themselves faithful in small matters will be among those whom God will promote to higher responsibilities (Matthew 25:21). **God's sovereignty shows his wise attention to detail.**

The tabernacle, and afterwards the temple, was the most important thing in the land, certainly as far as God was concerned. God established his sanctuary at Zion. It wasn't to be removed from there as it had been taken from Shiloh. The temple of God on Mount Zion at Jerusalem, the royal city, was to be a permanent institution. It's noteworthy that the building of the temple sanctuary is attributed to David here. He definitely had a desire to do so, and made preparations for it, as well as receiving the plan for it – but his son and successor, Solomon, was his agent in constructing it. And so, by the hand of David's son, the tabernacle gave place to its magnificent successor the temple, which remained with varying fortunes until it too came to an end as a result of human failure by David's successors.

David's time on the throne was a blessing to Israel. It's refreshing to read: *"He shepherded them according to the integrity of his heart; and guided them with his skillful hands."* There was no abuse of power. His administration was without corruption, and greatly benefitted the people under him. During his reign the kingdom became prosperous to an extent unknown before. In choosing a king for them, **God's sovereignty was for his people's prosperity.**

And David's example shows the truth recorded in the Book of Daniel where we read: *"the Most High is ruler over the realm of mankind and bestows it on whomever He wishes."* This agrees with what the prophet Isaiah says in Isaiah 40:23: *"He it is who reduces rulers to nothing, who makes the judges of the earth meaningless."* Because this is God's work, the Apostle Paul tells us: *"Every person is to be in subjection to the governing authorities. For there is no authority except from God, and those which exist are established by God. Therefore whoever resists authority has opposed the ordinance of God; and they who have opposed will receive condemnation upon themselves"* (Romans 13:1-2).

God's purposes cannot be thwarted by political campaigns, the ballot-box, or even force of arms. The counsel of Gamaliel could be applied as a warning against political activism: *"... if this plan or action is of men, it will be overthrown; but if it is of God, you will not be able to overthrow them; or else you may even be found fighting against God"* (Acts 5:38-39).

In concluding, let's come back to God's choice of David. Psalm 89 is another that stresses God's intervention in human affairs:

"I have exalted one chosen from the people. I have found David My servant; with My holy oil I have anointed him … I shall crush his adversaries before him, and strike those who hate him. My faithfulness and My lovingkindness will be with him … I also shall make him My firstborn, the highest of the kings of the earth" (Psalm 89:19-20, 23-24, 27).

It's certainly good news for Christians, for God's choice of David began a dynasty with eternal consequences: *"The gospel of God, which He promised beforehand … concerning His Son, who was born of a descendant of David"* (Romans 1:2-3).

7

GOD'S STRANGE WORK OF JUDGEMENT

The King James Version of the Bible describes certain actions by God as *"his strange work."* At Perazim, the LORD accomplished a great victory for Israel in the days of David (2 Samuel 5:20). At Gibeon, the LORD accomplished a great victory for Israel in the days of Joshua (Joshua 10:11). In those cases, the LORD fought *for* Israel, but if her leaders did not repent, they would soon find the LORD fighting *against* Israel. This use of God's strength against his people is, as the King James Version puts it, *his strange work*. This is how another version puts it: *"For the LORD will rise up as at Mount Perazim, He will be stirred up as in the valley of Gibeon, To do His task, His unusual task, And to work His work, His extraordinary work"* (Isaiah 28:21).

The strangeness of God's judgement against upon his own people was something the prophet Habakkuk struggled to understand or to get his head around, as we might say. The prophet Habakkuk's complaint to God initially was about the lawless state of his fellow-countrymen, the Jews. It seems then that law and order, even God's Law, in society around him had broken down. And so he prayed to God:

"How long, O LORD, will I call for help, And You will not hear? I cry out to You, "Violence!" Yet You do not save. Why do You make me see iniquity, and cause me to look on wickedness? Yes, destruction and violence are before me; strife exists and contention arises. Therefore the law is ignored and justice is never upheld. For the wicked surround the righteous; therefore justice comes out perverted" (Habakkuk 1:2-4).

Those words could have been written today, but they were written 2,500 years ago by a Bible prophet. It's been said that no other single issue keeps more people from God – or troubles them in their relationship with God - than the issue of suffering and injustice. Habakkuk, too, wondered why God allowed this to continue. He looked around the kingdom of Judah and cried out to God about the injustice and evil he saw everywhere. But no way was he prepared for God's response to his prayer. For God's answer to Habakkuk was:

"Look among the nations! Observe! Be astonished! Wonder! Because I am doing something in your days – you would not believe if you were told. For behold, I am raising up the Chaldeans, that fierce and impetuous people who march throughout the earth to seize dwelling places which are not theirs" (Habakkuk 1:5-6).

God answered Habakkuk, but it wasn't the response Habakkuk expected, nor even wanted to hear. In fact, it caused him to suffer more confusion. For God declares that he was raising up the Chaldeans - a fierce, cruel people - to execute judgment on Judah for their internal social injustice. That gave Habakkuk a bigger problem. He now struggled with how God could use those wicked oppressors to deal with the problems among his own people. And so Habakkuk's reaction to this was to say:

"You, O LORD, have appointed them to judge; And You, O Rock, have

established them to correct. Your eyes are too pure to approve evil, And You can not look on wickedness with favor. Why do You look with favor on those who deal treacherously? Why are You silent when the wicked swallow up those more righteous than they?" (Habakkuk 1:12-13).

In other words, he cried out to God again, asking how God could use one evil to correct another, lesser evil: *"Why are you silent while the wicked swallow up those more righteous than themselves?"* God responded a second time, declaring that he would bring all evil to account and settle every score. It might take longer than Habakkuk hoped, but God's justice would come decisively at the right time. Until then, he called on Habakkuk to trust him with the famous words: *"the righteous person will live by his or her faith."* Habakkuk questioned God's actions, but he accepted God's answer. Sceptical attitudes today lead people to go even further. Some even presume they can make better choices than God when they dare to play at being God.

In a Q & A session once, Christian apologist, Ravi Zacharias answered an enquirer by saying: "Can I ask you a question? On every university campus I visit, somebody stands up and says that God is an evil God to allow all this evil into our world. This person typically says, 'A plane crashes: Thirty people die, and twenty people live. What kind of a God would arbitrarily choose some to live and some to die?'" I continued, "but when we play God and determine whether a child within a mother's womb should live, we argue for that as a moral right. So when human beings are given the privilege of playing God, it's called a moral right. When God plays God, we call it an immoral act. Can you justify this for me?" That was the end of the conversation." He then commented further: "Does that not sound odd to you? When God decides who should live or die, he is immoral, when you decide who should live or die, it's your moral right. There was a pin-drop silence" (Ravi Zacharias, *The*

End of Reason, p.60).

And others today go even further. C.S. Lewis used to object to God's existence for this same reason - that reason being all the evil in the world. But then he realized something that many today have never wrestled with: how do I know things are evil or bad? His conclusion was that, in order to be able to recognize evil, he must have some standard of "good" against which he measures everything else. To use his illustration, one cannot recognize a crooked line unless he first has some concept of a straight one. But if there is no God, the very objection to evil loses its force, for if the universe is nothing but the result of random chance, then evil could never be recognized as such.

But returning to Habakkuk and his shocked reaction to God's chosen instrument of judgement. Remember that God had been explaining that he was going to use Israel's notoriously cruel and proud enemies, the Babylonians, to judge his own people, Israel.

"... Be astonished! Wonder! Because I am doing something in your days - You would not believe if you were told. For behold, I am raising up the Chaldeans, that fierce and impetuous people ... They are dreaded and feared; their justice and authority originate with themselves" (Habakkuk 1:5-7).

That led us to comment that God avenges wrongs and restores justice at times in strange ways. But who are we to criticise? God is sovereign. In the writings of the prophet Isaiah, I've been impressed all over again with its testimony to the sovereignty of God. Some statements repeat again and again such as: *"Who is like God?; Besides Him, there is no God; He is the Lord, there is no other."*

These statements teach us that God is sovereign, even if we don't understand how that works. Christians rely on the sovereignty of God to make prayer effective and to guarantee the success of evangelism. Only atheists can seriously claim not to believe in the sovereignty of God. Because if God isn't sovereign, then he's not God. As shocking as it was for Habakkuk to learn that the Babylonians would be God's instrument to judge; imagine the horror his fellow Israelites would have felt when the prophet Isaiah announced that God's chosen instrument to restore their fortunes after they'd been judged was another foreigner! As God promised to Habakkuk, the Babylonians in turn would be judged for their great wickedness. In his sovereignty, God was going to raise up the Persian Empire to put an end to Babylonian rule. Yes, a pagan messiah in the shape of the Persian Emperor Cyrus would capture the city of Babylon and free the Israelite people to return home to their land! Here's how Isaiah put it:

"Thus says the LORD to Cyrus His anointed, whom I have taken by the right hand, To subdue nations before him ... For the sake of Jacob My servant, and Israel My chosen one, I have also called you by your name; I have given you a title of honor though you have not known Me. I am the LORD, and there is no other; besides Me there is no God. I will gird you, though you have not known Me; ... "Woe to the one who quarrels with his Maker – an earthenware vessel among the vessels of earth! Will the clay say to the potter, 'What are you doing?' Or the thing you are making say, 'He has no hands?'" (Isaiah 45:1,4-5,9).

Notice that last verse about those quarrelling with their Maker? Surely, it's describing Jewish objections against the fact that God should choose and use a pagan king to be the one to ensure their safe passage back to Jerusalem. And it's too much that God should call this pagan 'his anointed.' This has to qualify as a strange work! After all, this is the same word 'messiah' used of the coming king who would belong to

David's dynasty. Perhaps it's a natural reaction to reject what we don't understand. Dylan, Nobel prize-winner for Literature (2016) inserted among his lyrical memory of the Titanic: "There is no understanding / For the judgment of God's hand."

It is safe to remember God's counsel through Isaiah: *"Will the clay say to the potter, 'What are you doing?'"* God is the potter, and we are the clay. Nothing that happens is free from the sovereignty of God. There is no injustice with God. *"Ascribe greatness to our God! ... His work is perfect. ... All His ways are just"* (Deuteronomy 32:4). Judgement may seem strange to us, but we can be assured it is perfect and just.

8

THE ANOINTING OF A PAGAN MESSIAH, CYRUS

The British Museum in London contains the cylinder of Cyrus. It documents Cyrus, the Emperor of Persia, conquering Babylon without a battle and speaks of his permitting the return of Israel to their homeland. In more detail, it tells of how Cyrus was: "allowed ... to enter Babylon without battle or fight, sparing his own city of Babylon from hardship ... I returned to these sanctuaries on the other side of the Tigris, sanctuaries founded in ancient times, the images that had been in them there and I made their dwellings permanent. I also gathered all their people and returned to them their habitations" (https://www.britishmuseum.org/collection/object/W_1880-0617-1941).

There are two remarkable things there, quite extraordinary in fact. First, that the seemingly invincible Babylon should have been captured without a fight. How could that happen? We'll return to that shortly. But, the other noteworthy feature contained in the decree on the cylinder of Cyrus is the fact that he reversed his empire's time-honoured foreign policy. It had long been the conventional wisdom that the way to prevent conquered lands from rebelling was to strictly impose a forced migration policy on all of its nobility. If all its movers and shakers were transported to other lands, there was much less risk of anyone remaining behind who was able to plan a revolt. Strategically, this made good sense, and had proved very effective. Why reverse it at this stage? We'll also be returning to that, because it shows clearly the working of the divine hand that moves the world, including its superpowers.

Let's use our Bibles to check out how God had announced this shock defeat and sea-change of policy many years in advance. The Book of Isaiah is one of the most admired books of the Bible. The New Testament writers quote Isaiah more than any of the other Old Testament prophets. From a literary point of view, the writing of Isaiah is superb. But beyond his writing skill, Isaiah's book is filled with prophecies about God's people and the surrounding nations (and it also contains lots of Messianic prophecies - see Isaiah 7:14-16; 9:1-7; 11:1-16; 32:1ff; 42:1-7; 50:5-8; 52:13-15; 53:1-12; 61:1-3; 65:17 - even describing Jesus' crucifixion in detail 700 years before it happened).

Many Bible commentators fail to glimpse the awesome greatness of God and so they post-date prophecies by reading them as retrospective histories long after the event. Nothing could be further from the truth. In fact, this is precisely the point at issue in the debate God sets up in a mock courtroom scene described for us by the prophet Isaiah. It's as if the LORD, the God of Israel, calls on his people, Israel, to be his witnesses in a court of law. Arranged against him are the nations and their gods. Decisive evidence is required as to who is the true god. And the evidence presented by Israel's God is his ability to predict the future:

'"Present your case,' the LORD says. 'Bring forward your strong arguments,' the King of Jacob says. 'Let them bring forth and declare to us what is going to take place; as for the former events, declare what they were, that we may consider them and know their outcome. Or announce to us what is coming; declare the things that are going to come afterward, that we may know that you are gods; indeed, do good or evil, that we may anxiously look about us and fear together. Behold, you are of no account, and your work amounts to nothing; he who chooses you is an abomination. I have aroused one from the north, and he has come; from the rising of the sun he will call on My name; and he will come upon rulers as upon mortar, even as the potter treads clay. Who has declared this from the beginning, that we might know? Or from former times, that we may say, 'He is right!'? Surely there was no one who declared, surely there was no one who proclaimed, surely there was no one who heard your words" (Isaiah 41:21-26).

As Israel's God, he confronts the gods of the nations in a virtual courtroom battle, calling on them to "*present their case*" and their "*strong arguments*" (Isaiah 41:21-24). From the north and east, he was bringing a deliverer for Zion, announcing this before Judah even went into the captivity from which they were to be delivered (Isaiah 41:25-26)! On the other side of the court, all his opponents and would-be rivals are silent and impotent. None of them could do the same. Later in chapters 44 and 45, the LORD gives more detail of his telling of the future:

"[God says] 'It is I who says of Jerusalem, "She shall be inhabited!" And of the cities of Judah, "They shall be built." And I will raise up her ruins again ... It is I who says of Cyrus, 'He is My shepherd! And he will perform all My desire.' And he declares of Jerusalem, 'She will be built,' And of the temple, 'Your foundation will be laid.'"

"Thus says the LORD to Cyrus His anointed, Whom I have taken by the right hand, To subdue nations before him and to loose the loins of kings; to open doors before him so that gates will not be shut: I will go before you and make *the rough places smooth; I will shatter the doors of bronze and cut through their iron bars. I will give you the treasures of darkness and hidden wealth of secret places, so that you may know that it is I, the LORD, the God of Israel, who calls you by your name. For the sake of Jacob My servant, and Israel My chosen one, I have also called you by your name; I have given you a title of honor though you have not known Me. I am the LORD, and there is no other; besides Me there is no God. I will gird you, though you have not known Me. That men may know from the rising to the setting of the sun that there is no one besides Me. I am the LORD, and there is no other"* (Isaiah 44:26,28; 45:1-6).

Cyrus, king of the Persian city of Anshan, ascended to power in 559BC. Ten years later he killed the rival king of the Median people, established the Persian Empire and extended it from modern Turkey as far as India. When he took Babylon in 539BC, he reversed the policy of previous empires. Far from transporting subdued peoples, he encouraged them to go home – and this applied to Israelites, confirmed by the cylinder in the London museum.

Let's rewind to 539BC. Instead of preparing to meet the Persian threat to his kingdom, Babylon's king has decided to throw a party for a thousand of his lords. To some extent, Belshazzar's overconfidence is understandable. Babylon was square, about 15 miles on each side. It boasted an outside wall 87 feet wide. Herodotus talks of chariot races around the wall six abreast! Inside this wall was a second wall, with a moat, a water defence, between them – oh, and 250 watchtowers! The river Euphrates crossed the city, providing the water for both the protective moat and for survival purposes during a siege. Babylon was widely regarded as impregnable.

But Herodotus describes how the Persians diverted the river Euphrates into a canal up-river so that the water level dropped 'to the height of the middle of a man's thigh,' which made the flood defences useless and enabled the invaders to march along the river-bed to enter by night. The way of conquest was virtually bloodless, with no significant damage to the city.

But while still feeling secure, earlier on the very night this happened, the Babylonian king Belshazzar had in the festivities desecrated the vessels that had been taken from the Jewish Temple, captured by Nebuchadnezzar 70 years earlier. But he was shocked to see some writing appearing on the plaster of the wall of the king's palace. This historic incident, recorded in graphic detail in the pages of the Bible, has given us our modern expression of 'the writing on the wall' whenever we think of an early indication of some impending failure. God's servant, Daniel, among the captives of Israel held in Babylon, interpreted the written message for the king. It sealed his fate. The city would fall that night in the way we described. And Daniel also had a message from God for the incoming king.

Perhaps, we can imagine how, after Cyrus' triumphal entry into the city, Daniel could have presented to Cyrus the writings of Isaiah that included the letter we quoted (Isaiah 44 and 45), addressed to Cyrus by name, and written 150 years earlier. Daniel might even have said to Cyrus: 'I've been waiting for you!' Having been called by name in a letter written before he was born, Cyrus would realize this was from God. He must have been astonished! Was this a factor in him arranging for the Hebrew captives to be permitted to return to Jerusalem? So, the Jews were encouraged by Cyrus to return and rebuild their temple (see Ezra 1).

These two events - the taking of Babylon without a battle and the unprecedented freeing of the Jews soon after - are both remarkable historical events in themselves. What makes them even more notable is the fact that God foretold this destiny in Isaiah's prophecy, mentioning Cyrus by name 100 years before his birth. As shocking as it was for Habakkuk to learn that the Babylonians would be God's instrument to judge; imagine the horror for them (captured in Isaiah 45:9) when Isaiah announces a pagan messiah in the shape of Cyrus (Isaiah 45:1)! But such are the sovereign workings of almighty God. We stand in awe!

9

UNSCRIPTED PREPARATIONS FOR THE FULLNESS OF THE TIME

The Gospels open the New Testament by announcing that the fullness of time had come (Mark 1:15). God was about to reveal his Messiah to the world. Prior to this, the Old Testament records the time in which God was preparing the world for the coming of his son. As Paul would later say, the Jewish Law, given through Moses, was to be like a tutor leading a pupil to the Messiah (Galatians 3:24). Then, *"when the fullness of the time came"* (Galatians 4:4), God sent his son. His coming would end 400 years of silence between Old and New Testaments.

First, let's rewind a little. The reconstruction of the walls of Jerusalem was completed in 444BC under the leadership of Nehemiah. After that, the exiles who'd returned from captivity in Babylon struggled to survive in the ancient Near East. This was because their land was a hotly contested land-bridge between major military powers in the region.

Still, the 400 years between the prophet Malachi and the birth of Christ were important years in the history of Israel. During them, the Israel nation witnessed the fall of the Persian Empire, the rise and fall of the Greek Empire, and the rise of the Roman Empire; not only witnessed, but they were caught up in these happenings. It's the hallmark of deity that God can write up the future just as easily as the past. The 11th chapter of the Book of the prophet Daniel begins:

"... Behold, three more kings are going to arise in Persia. Then a fourth will gain far more riches than all of them; as soon as he becomes strong through his riches, he will arouse the whole empire against the realm of Greece. And a mighty king will arise, and he will rule with great authority and do as he pleases. But as soon as he has arisen, his kingdom will be broken up ..." (Daniel 11:2-4).

Daniel is informed that the present leadership in the Persian Empire would be succeeded by four rulers. Xerxes, the fourth, was the most influential, and during his reign he fought wars against Greece. The *"mighty king"* who would arise was Alexander the Great. The Persian Empire remained the dominant power in the Ancient Near East until in 331BC it was conquered by Alexander the Great. Alexander was the son of Philip of Macedon and the pupil of the Greek philosopher Aristotle, just as Aristotle had been the pupil of Plato and Plato the pupil of Socrates.

Scientists and philosophers accompanied Alexander in his conquest of the ancient world in order to help Aristotle try to unify all branches of knowledge. Throughout his empire, Alexander emphasized Hellenism, which was the spread of Greek language and culture. This was to prepare the way for the New Testament to be written in Greek.

After the death of Alexander, the Grecian empire later came to be divided between two main dynasties, one ruling Egypt to the south (the Ptolemies) and the other to the north of Israel ruling Syrian and modern

Turkey (the Seleucids). After initial conquest of Israel by the Egypt-based dynasty, the northern dynasty, with its strong Greek influence, took over Israel in 198BC. Its leader at that time began to accelerate the process of Hellenization in Israel. This was fiercely opposed by conservative Jews. The Hassidim, or 'pious ones,' fought in vain against the growing Greek influence on the Jews. Many groups struggled to maintain the purity of their traditions, including the Pharisees who appear frequently in the New Testament. The Pharisees or 'separated ones' were zealous for the covenant and tried to be obedient to every aspect of the law, but they'd degenerated into self-righteous legalism and ritualism by the time of Christ in the Gospels.

The next section (vv.5-20) of the long eleventh chapter of Daniel describes the conflicts between succeeding kings of these regional powers to the north and south of Israel. During all this, the land of Israel was invaded first by one power and then by the other. Although we've no time to examine the details, every scriptural statement made in this section has had its precise fulfilment in history. In the first 35 verses of Daniel 11, some 135 predictions were made which were all subsequently realized historically.

Then the spotlight falls dramatically on one leader, named in history as Antiochus IV Epiphanes (175-164BC), who became the king of the northern power in 175BC. He considered himself a god and ended his years in insanity. This man began a radically anti-Jewish program in Palestine and was nicknamed Antiochus Epimanes, which means "madman."

When he experienced setbacks at the hand of his southern rival, Antiochus took out his frustration on the Jews, the city of Jerusalem, and their temple. After all, Israel's territory lay between the two hostile kings.

He vented his fury against the law of Moses, desecrated the temple, and put a stop to the daily sacrifice. Here's what the prophet Daniel had predicted:

"Forces from him will arise, desecrate the sanctuary fortress, and do away with the regular sacrifice. And they will set up the abomination of desolation. By smooth words he will turn to godlessness those who act wickedly toward the covenant, but the people who know their God will display strength and take action" (Daniel 11:31-32).

In trying to get rid of Judaism and enforce Greek culture on the Jews, Antiochus banned the Jews from following their religious practices and ordered copies of the Law to be burned. Worst of all, on December 16, 167BC he built an altar to Zeus on the altar of burnt offering outside the Jewish temple, and offered a pig on it. He fulfilled the Old Testament prophecy about setting up the *"abomination that makes desolate"* (see also Daniel 9:27; Matthew 24:15).

We note in passing that our Lord later referred to this same prophecy of Daniel. The fact he did so, makes it clear that it remains to be most fully fulfilled in the future (even beyond any further possible partial fulfilment in AD70). This will be when the 'man of lawlessness,' a.k.a the anti-Christ, will set himself up in the rebuilt Jerusalem Temple (2 Thessalonians 2:4). The later verses of Daniel chapter 11 were not historically fulfilled in Antiochus Epiphanes, but from v.35 onwards (note 'the end time'), they point to the future anti-Christ figure he prefigured, and of whom the Bible elsewhere speaks (e.g. Revelation 13:6). Such progressive fulfilment of Bible prophecy is not uncommon, and what seems like history repeating itself is but the pattern of divine providence.

Antiochus promised apostate Jews great reward if they would set aside their God and instead worship the god of Greece. Many were persuaded by his flattering promises and worshipped the false god. But a small remnant remained faithful. The Jews who refused to submit to Antiochus' false religious system were persecuted and martyred. In 166BC, a man by the name of Mattathias refused to submit to this false religious system. He and his sons fled from Jerusalem to the mountains and began the Maccabean revolt in 164BC. The Maccabean family launched a guerrilla war against the forces of Antiochus. After the death of Mattathias, leadership of the revolt fell to his third son, Judas "the Hammer" Maccabeus. The Maccabean revolt succeeded in securing concessions from Antiochus, including religious freedom and opening the temple for religious ceremonies. The reopening and rededication of the temple is still commemorated today in the Jewish holiday of Hanukkah.

The Jews secured their freedom in 142BC from foreign powers and remained independent until 63BC when the Romans conquered them under the command of Pompey. Pompey was a member of Rome's first great triumvirate. An Idumean (Edomite) chieftain named Herod the Great was appointed as a local king over the Jews in 40BC. He founded a dynasty and rebuilt the Jerusalem temple, having been appointed by Mark Antony and Octavius (perhaps more famously known as Caesar Augustus).

And so, the New Testament opens with the Jewish people under the domination of the Romans and an oppressive king. But, in the bigger picture, the whole Roman empire was under the protection of Roman law. The Romans built roads all over their empire in order to quickly transport their troops from one place to another. Christians would come to use these roads to take the gospel easily to the four corners of the empire, and they were able to do it fairly safely because the roads were protected by Roman troops.

So, this was a time perfectly suited – in the sovereign providence of almighty God – for the introduction of the gospel. "There was now nothing to prevent the preacher of a new faith going from city to city and country to country ... It was 'due time' for Christ to be born" (Romans 5:6, J.C. Ryle, Gospel of Luke)

As we've seen, Alexander had earlier extended Greek civilization in the then known world. God had spread a language that was to become the vehicle of the gospel, the Greek language. The books of the New Testament were originally written in Greek. And so, the Apostle Paul could later stand and speak one language in Israel, Syria, Turkey, Greece, Italy, and wherever else he ventured – and be understood by all.

What's more, Rome did spread law and order. Her strength lay in the area of executive power and organization. She gave a system of government and justice to every people, tribe and nation of the known world. Also, as we said, the Romans famously built roads that allowed commerce and communication. God would seem to have made sure of that, because over those roads the gospel was to go to the hinterlands. Under Rome's influence a form of civilized peace held sway.

With resilient Judaism, faithful at its core, and fired with messianic expectation; with the Greek legacy of a rich language and enquiring minds; and with the Roman ongoing contribution of organized travel routes with relatively peaceful law and order – we can fully appreciate that the fullness of the time had come (Galatians 4:4). It was then, as planned, that God sent his son.

10

THE DEATH OF CHRIST AS SOMETHING FORE-ORDAINED

I read of a boy growing up in Britain during the Second World War who soon became aware of how the early days of the war were full of doom and gloom. British forces had to withdraw from Europe. German bombers filled the skies. Survival was marginal. The British Isles were threatened with invasion, its navy being sunk faster than ships could be replaced. But the news broadcasts over the BBC – even amid all the bad news – kept repeating one reassuring sentence: 'Everything is proceeding according to plan.' The boy in our story remembered well his reaction: 'Whose plan?' 'We need a better one!' But despite appearances, the plan worked.

God, too, had a plan. It involved sending Jesus into this world and to the city of Jerusalem almost 2,000 years ago. Despite appearances at the time, that plan also worked. Paul's letter to the Ephesians gives us this reassuring sentence, that all was *"in accordance with the eternal purpose which He carried out in Christ Jesus our Lord"* (Ephesians 3:11).

In the counsels of eternity, God the Son joyfully signed his own death warrant, meaning that one day as the man Christ Jesus he would go to the cross and die. It was all planned. Not only were we (believers) chosen in Christ *"before the foundation of the world"* (Ephesians 1:4), but Christ himself is described as the Lamb slain from the foundation of the world, as John adds in the Book of Revelation (Revelation 13:8).

The decision to create a habitable universe for humanity was thoroughly costed when the Father, Son and Spirit took counsel together in eternity. If they were to act in the creation of this magnificent universe, then they'd inevitably also have to prepare in advance a work of restoration – at least they would if their creation was to be endowed with a freewill, which it was. This brings us to three verses which flow from the Apostle Peter's 'pen.'

"... knowing that you were not redeemed with perishable things like silver or gold from your futile way of life inherited from your forefathers, but with precious blood, as of a lamb unblemished and spotless, the blood of Christ. For He was foreknown before the foundation of the world, but has appeared in these last times for the sake of you" (1 Peter 1:18-20).

The Father in eternity gave the Son people whom the Spirit would eventually unite to him in history. Jesus very clearly says this in his John 17 prayer. In verse 9, Jesus clarifies that the prayer he's offering is not *"on behalf of the world, but of those whom You have given Me,"* saying this to his Father, of course. This is an idea repeated many times in Christ's prayer, that both his prayer and work is on behalf of those whom the Father has given to him, not everyone. The culmination of Christ's work was the cross. That foul event was permitted in God's sovereign purpose. It was the most vital part of God's predetermined plan. It was totally successful according to all God's intention. Here are some words from the Apostle Peter:

"Men of Israel, listen to these words: Jesus the Nazarene, a man attested to you by God with miracles and wonders and signs which God performed through Him in your midst, just as you yourselves know - this Man, delivered over by the predetermined plan and foreknowledge of God, you nailed to a cross by the hands of godless men and put Him to death. But God raised Him up again, putting an end to the agony of death, since it was impossible for Him to be held in its power" (Acts 2:22-24).

There was nothing incidental, far less accidental, in anything that surrounded the crucifixion of our Lord. Pontius Pilate, the Roman governor in charge of proceedings, might make the claim to Christ: *'I have authority to release You,'* but Jesus could truly counter: *'You would have no authority over Me, unless it had been given you from above; for this reason he who delivered Me to you has the greater sin.'* These words not only proclaim God's absolute sovereignty over the events of that day, but also don't relieve the perpetrators of their human responsibility. Even the detailed manner of Christ's betrayal was part of the plan that worked. On one occasion, it's recorded that Jesus answered his disciples, saying:

"Jesus answered them, 'Did I Myself not choose you, the twelve, and yet one of you is a devil?' Now He meant Judas the son of Simon Iscariot, for he, one of the twelve, was going to betray Him" (John 6:70-71).

When choosing the Twelve, the Lord had deliberately chosen Judas, fully aware, of course, that his character was devilish, and this would lead him to betray him. And so the scene was set for what is commonly called 'the Last Supper':

"As they were eating, He said, 'Truly I say to you that one of you will betray Me.' Being deeply grieved, they each one began to say to Him, 'Surely not I, Lord?' And He answered, 'He who dipped his hand with Me in the bowl

is the one who will betray Me. The Son of Man is to go, just as it is written of Him; but woe to that man by whom the Son of Man is betrayed! It would have been good for that man if he had not been born.' And Judas, who was betraying Him, said, 'Surely it is not I, Rabbi?' Jesus said to him, 'You have said it yourself'" (Matthew 26:21-24).

Before the plan had formed in Judas' mind, every detail was known to the Lord, and was in total agreement with what the Old Testament part of the Bible had predicted (Psalm 109:8). Jesus referred to this in his John 17 prayer: *"While I was with them, I was keeping them in Your name which You have given Me; and I guarded them and not one of them perished but the son of perdition, so that the Scripture would be fulfilled"* (John 17:12).

And after Christ's resurrection, Peter was once again the spokesman who said to the others:

"Brethren, the Scripture had to be fulfilled, which the Holy Spirit foretold by the mouth of David concerning Judas, who became a guide to those who arrested Jesus. For he was counted among us and received his share in this ministry ... *"For it is written in the book of Psalms ... 'LET ANOTHER MAN TAKE HIS OFFICE'"* (Acts 1:16-17, 20).

And so they appointed a replacement. Now, to conclude our consideration of how everything about the cross happened according to plan, I want us to explore its timing. Matthew, in his Gospel, tells us:

"When Jesus had finished all these words, He said to His disciples, 'You know that after two days the Passover is coming, and the Son of Man is to be handed over for crucifixion.' Then the chief priests and the elders of the people were gathered together in the court of the high priest, named Caiaphas; and they plotted together to seize Jesus by stealth and kill Him. But they were saying,

'Not during the festival, otherwise a riot might occur among the people'" (Matthew 26:1,3-5).

Notice how those plotting Jesus' death, had discounted making their move at the Jewish festival of Passover, but Jesus informed his followers that Passover would, in fact, be the time. The big picture of the Bible reveals his death had to be at Jerusalem (Luke 13:33). And equally, that same big picture, pinpointed the exact moment in history when it would take place – the year, the month, the day, even the hour. The analogy of the Jewish Passover ritual and the revelation of God's program given to the prophet Daniel taken together allow us to see this precise level of detail.

God had shared with Daniel, in chapters 2 and 7, his plan for the Gentile world at large, in terms of the 4 great successive empires from the time of the 6th century BC right through until the time of Christ's return to earth to set up his kingdom. In chapter 9 of Daniel, God now shares with his servant his plan for Daniel's own people, the Jewish people:

"Seventy weeks have been decreed for your people and your holy city ... from the issuing of a decree to restore and rebuild Jerusalem until Messiah the Prince there will be seven weeks and sixty-two weeks ... Then after the sixty-two weeks the Messiah will be cut off and have nothing ..." (Daniel 9:24-26).

Seventy 'weeks' are literally seventy 'sevens' where each 'seven' is a unit of seven years. These are prophetic years each of 360 days (by comparison with the 70th 'week' in Revelation 11:2; 12:6,14; 13:5), which makes the time interval described as a total of 69 weeks to be 476 ordinary solar years - stretching from the restoration of the city by the completion of its wall by Nehemiah in 444 BC - all the way to the cross of Christ in AD33 (see Dating the Crucifixion, Colin J. Humphreys

& W.G. Waddington, *Nature* volume 306, pages 743–746, 1983). From 444BC to AD33 is 476 years. What's more, the Messiah would die at the precise time of the killing of the Passover lambs that year (in one of the two systems then in vogue for reckoning it). Jesus and his disciples celebrated Passover at the time the Galileans did, a full 24 hours ahead of the Judean custom. And that, too, is the wonderful sovereignty of God in the detail. That there were two such systems side by side allowed Jesus to both observe the Passover and also fulfill it (H.W. Hoehner, Chronological Aspects ..., CEP,1977).

Finally, the Bible records, and history confirms, that the birth and death of Jesus Christ was marked by signs in the skies, involving the moon and stars (Matthew 2:2; Acts 2:20). The movement of these heavenly bodies is regular, like a great clock, following laws which are known to us. It's wonderful to think of how in the act of bringing the universe into existence, God 'set the clock' for the moment his son would enter human history in the person of Jesus of Nazareth. He marked it in the stars. And from before the beginning of time, God also 'set the clock' for the very moment when Jesus, his Son, as man, would expire on the cross, in terms of the lunar eclipse which occurred then. A lunar eclipse which caused the moon to be seen as blood red in colour from Jerusalem (Phlegon Trallianus, Olympiades etc.). This further testifies that Jesus is "the Lamb that was slain from the creation of the world" (Revelation 13:8) – and that absolutely everything proceeded 'according to plan.'

11

THE SETTING ASIDE OF ISRAEL TO BRING IN GENTILES

God's Good News of salvation was always intended to be for the Jew first, but it was never intended to be for the Jew only. The martyrdom of Stephen, as recorded in Acts chapter 7, was a crisis in the post-Pentecost period. Jerusalem witnessed no public miracle after that, only Peter's nocturnal release from prison (Acts 12).

The Spirit of God had descended at Pentecost in manifest power, and although large numbers had afterwards believed, there was no national repentance. The Son of God had interceded for those who had rejected him; but rejection of the Spirit of God was unacceptable. Jerusalem was ground zero of the Gospel-rejection that spread outwards among Jews as the effects of Gospel preaching widened, when Paul rather than Peter would become its chief evangelist.

God shook the Philippian jail when Paul was imprisoned overnight there, but heaven was conspicuously silent when he was later confined in Rome awaiting Nero's pleasure. At that stage, the Gospel was being disseminated globally from the heart of the empire. It was after Paul had drawn a clear line in the sand as recorded in Acts chapter 28:

"When they had set a day for Paul, they came to him at his lodging in large numbers; and he was explaining to them by solemnly testifying about the kingdom of God and trying to persuade them concerning Jesus, from both the Law of Moses and from the Prophets, from morning until evening. Some were being persuaded by the things spoken, but others would not believe. And when they did not agree with one another, they began leaving after Paul had spoken one parting word, 'The Holy Spirit rightly spoke through Isaiah the prophet to your fathers, saying, "GO TO THIS PEOPLE AND SAY, 'YOU WILL KEEP ON HEARING, BUT WILL NOT UNDERSTAND; AND YOU WILL KEEP ON SEEING, BUT WILL NOT PERCEIVE; FOR THE HEART OF THIS PEOPLE HAS BECOME DULL, AND WITH THEIR EARS THEY SCARCELY HEAR, AND THEY HAVE CLOSED THEIR EYES; OTHERWISE THEY MIGHT SEE WITH THEIR EYES, AND HEAR WITH THEIR EARS, AND UNDERSTAND WITH THEIR HEART AND RETURN, AND I WOULD HEAL THEM.' Therefore let it be known to you that this salvation of God has been sent to the Gentiles; they will also listen" (Acts 28:23-28).

As the Apostolic era came to an end, this signalled a sea-change. The phase of Jewish precedence or primacy was over. When the Jews rejected the message, the signs and wonders ceased. From the time of the Exodus, and when they'd occurred for a limited period afterwards, they'd always been a witness to the Jewish people. As the thrust of global evangelism turned outward to the Gentile world, the signs and wonders ceased, towards the end of the Apostolic era. The Gospel was no longer in its 'Jew first' mode.

This was all in God's programming of events. Isaiah (chapter 28) and Joel (chapter 2) had spoken of the signs by which God would testify to his ancient people. Signs had occurred before, of course. The sign of tongues was first a reference to the foreign language spoken by the Babylonians through whom God spoke in judgement to his people, Israel. Thousands upon thousands of Jews had been reached with Christianity, but it could never be all Israel who would receive this revelation of the arm of the Lord (Isaiah 53:1). For Israel nationally was destined to stumble (1 Peter 2:8). That fact was included in their destiny.

At the beginning of the 25th chapter of Jeremiah the prophet, there stands recorded the first Gentile date in the whole Bible, and that is the first year of Nebuchadnezzar. What had happened? Why this sudden Gentile time reference? God's chosen people, Israel, had stumbled and fallen away from faith and privilege. Chronic disobedience had robbed them of special nation status. And so had begun *"the times of the Gentiles"* (Luke 21:24). This date in the 7th century BC, unheralded as it is in history, is in reality one of the most significant dates in history. God revealed to the Bible prophet, Daniel, its enormous significance. We don't learn about it in school, but this date is of the utmost importance. For Israel had been relegated from the top spot in world affairs. Starting with Babylonians, then Medo-Persians and the Greeks, no less than four mighty empires would hold sway over the world while Israel would languish.

However, God wasn't finished with Israel – and he still isn't. The Good News for Jews was that a future king of David's dynasty would restore Israel's fortunes some time way in the future. This was all made known in advance through the Bible prophet Daniel (chapters 2 and 7). But the way back wouldn't be a smooth one. Israel would fail to recognise her deliverer, her Messiah. Isaiah the prophet had spelt this out most clearly in his 53rd chapter. The Apostle Peter takes up words from Psalm 118 (already applied to Jesus 3 times in the New Testament), and showed Israel was destined to reject her Messiah at first sight. The cross was no mistake or accident, nor was it without meaning for God. On the contrary, all his purposes depended on it. Here are the Apostle Peter's words taken from his first Bible letter, chapter two:

"For it stands in Scripture: 'Behold, I am laying in Zion a stone, a cornerstone chosen and precious, and whoever believes in him will not be put to shame.' So the honor is for you who believe, but for those who do not believe, 'The stone that the builders rejected has become the cornerstone,' and 'A stone of stumbling, and a rock of offense.' They stumble because they disobey the word, as they were destined to do. But you are a chosen race, a royal priesthood, a holy nation, a people for his own possession, that you may proclaim the excellencies of him who called you out of darkness into his marvelous light. Once you were not a people, but now you are God's people; once you had not received mercy, but now you have received mercy" (1 Peter 2:6-10 ESV).

In order to bring in the Gentiles, it was within God's sovereign plan that Israel would be disobedient. Peter is quoting the Bible prophet Hosea at that point. God's command to Hosea was most challenging. He was told to marry one who (at best interpretation) would soon turn out to be a prostitute. There may have been a cruel irony in the name of the third mentioned child after their marriage, Lo-Ammi. Perhaps this son really was not the son of Hosea, but of another man. Perhaps the appearance of the child made this evident. The message God had to deliver to Israel through Hosea was hard enough, but God also made Hosea to *live* it. If this is correct, then the one who was no son was commanded by God to be taken as a son.

And so the meaning was: God's unfaithful people, Israel, who had made themselves not to be God's people, would in God's amazing grace be taken again as his people. Hosea's words had meaning for his family life, but they also had meaning for the fate of the nation – they would go as captives into Babylon but would return again to Jerusalem. But there's more! By the Spirit of God, the Apostle Peter applies the text globally. What he's saying is that Gentiles were once not God's people, but those to whom Peter was writing had by God's grace become God's people. What does that mean for Israel now? The Apostle Paul takes up this question: *"I ask, then, has God rejected his people? By no means! For I myself am an Israelite, a descendant of Abraham, a member of the tribe of Benjamin. God has not rejected his people whom he foreknew ..."* (Romans 11:1-2).

In effect, Paul is saying God had temporarily rejected Israel, but not absolutely. They were only set aside for a definite period in God's sovereign dealings with them. For what reason?

"... through their trespass salvation has come to the Gentiles, so as to make Israel jealous. Now ... if their failure means riches for the Gentiles, how much more will their full inclusion mean! For if their rejection means the reconciliation of the world, what will their acceptance mean but life from the dead?" (Romans 11:11-12, 15).

Notice there, it's rejection of Israel followed by acceptance again of Israel. And between their being rejected and their being accepted again lies the whole Church Age we're living in; a period when God's offer of salvation is being preached to the whole – and mainly Gentile – world. So, Israel's rejection by God has blessed the Gentiles, and Paul implies that Israel's future acceptance by God will bring even greater blessings. He signs off by emphasizing God's sovereignty:

"... a partial hardening has come upon Israel, until the fullness of the Gentiles has come in. And in this way all Israel will be saved ... For just as you were at one time disobedient to God but now have received mercy because of

their disobedience, so they too have now been disobedient in order that by the mercy shown to you they also may now receive mercy. For God has consigned all to disobedience, that he may have mercy on all. [And here we join with Paul in saying:] *Oh, the depth of the riches both of the wisdom and knowledge of God!"* (Romans 11:25-26, 30-33).

12

MANAGING THE WORLD

Anyone who's had the slightest interest in American politics has surely got used to the way the word 'Administration' is used over there. You might read about, for example, 'the Clinton Administration' and hear it contrasted with 'the Obama Administration.' Each incoming President puts his own team in place and policies begin to take their distinctive shape. The way each president runs things is different from the way his predecessors did it.

I mention that because it's possible to read the Bible and see this whole world as a household run by God, with God as its administrator. That way of viewing things is encouraged by finding the word *oikonomia* in our Bibles (literally 'the law of the house or household.') This word, often translated as 'stewardship,' means 'an administration,' whether of a house, or property or a nation - or as we're thinking of it - as the administration of the human race or any part of it, at any given time. Just as a parent would govern his household in different ways, according to varying needs at different times, so God has at different times dealt with humanity in different ways, but always overall for his glory.

In his 'household-world,' God is seen to be stewarding or administering its affairs as he himself chooses, and in various stages of revelation as time progresses. These various stages are what we might call different 'economies' in the outworking of God's total purpose. And these different economies form the 'administrations' or 'dispensations.' The understanding of God's differing economies is essential to a proper interpretation of his revelation within them. For one thing, it helps us to see how God's plans for the Church (the Body of Christ) don't replace his separate plans for the nation of Israel.

And so there's another idea that's important for understanding the Bible and the God of the Bible: it's what's been called 'progressive revelation.' Progressive revelation is the recognition that God's message to us – his truth - was not given all at once, but unpacked in a series of stages. The varying stages of revelation show God working in different ways (with different 'covenants') at different times. Spotting this allows us to divide the history of the world into separate 'administrations.' It can be helpful to arrange the stages of divine revelation into this sequence of 'dispensations' – as they're often termed. In biblical use, a *dispensation* is the stewardship of a particular revelation of God's purposes, and this in turn brings added responsibility to those to whom the revelation is given by God. Each stage adds to the whole body of truth for which humans are responsible in the gradual unfolding revelation of God's purpose in salvation.

The principle of progressive revelation is really quite obvious straight from the pages of our Bible. Paul told his audience on Mars Hill that in a former day God had overlooked their ignorance, but now he commands repentance (Acts 17:30). And again, the majestic opening of the book of Hebrews outlines the progressive revelation (Hebrews 1:1,2) by means of prophets before Christ came. Another example may be found in Jesus telling his followers that he was going away but another helper, the Holy Spirit, would come and from then on the Spirit would not only remain with them but be internal to them (John 14:16,17; 14:26; and 16:24). That was the dramatic difference Pentecost would make. That's one of the changepoints of the differing administrations we've been talking about. As we've seen there, the main points of change between differing stages in the progressive revelation of truth to us by God are made quite plain by the Bible itself. Let's start near to the beginning of recorded history, with the Apostle Paul saying:

"Therefore, just as through one man sin entered into the world, and death through sin, and so death spread to all men, because all sinned – for until the Law sin was in the world, but sin is not imputed when there is no law. Nevertheless death reigned from Adam until Moses, even over those who had not sinned in the likeness of the offense of Adam, who is a type of Him who was to come" (Romans 5:12-14).

That's fairly obvious, isn't it? 'From Adam until Moses,' was the period of early history before God gave detailed laws, before the Ten Commandments. The Lord Jesus himself clarifies the total extent of the period during which the Law of Moses characterized God's dealings with men and women, when he said: *"The Law and the Prophets were proclaimed until John; since that time the gospel of the kingdom of God has been preached, and everyone is forcing his way into it"* (Luke 16:16).

Now, John the Baptist was the Lord's forerunner, and one of the most striking verses that shows the different ways of God's dealing with the world of men and women is found in John 1:17: *"For the Law was given through Moses; grace and truth were realized through Jesus Christ."* That clear statement in the prologue to John's Gospel marks out for us how dramatically the divine economy changed with the coming of

Christ. Of course, we really shouldn't expect anything else to be the case. The way God managed his relationship with the world of humans was revolutionized at that time.

But let me make this clear: it wasn't that there was one way of salvation from eternal damnation in the Old Testament and a different one from New Testament times onwards. That's not what we're saying. Abraham and David etc. were saved by faith just as we are (see Romans chapter 4). But the Law acted like a tutor, Paul says in Galatians (chapter 3), to bring people to Christ, the Jews particularly. During the period of the Law, God was revealing how serious a problem sin is; and its sacrificial system was intended to help us to understand the necessity of Christ's sacrifice on the cross. Then the cross would usher in yet another new administration of God's dealings with humanity, and it was to the Apostle Paul that clear insight was given about this. This is him sharing this momentous fact with the local church of God at Ephesus:

"To me, the very least of all saints, this grace was given, to preach to the Gentiles the unfathomable riches of Christ, and to bring to light what is the administration of the mystery which for ages has been hidden in God who created all things; so that the manifold wisdom of God might now be made known through the church to the rulers and the authorities in the heavenly places" (Ephesians 3:8-10).

Those are words we need to reflect on. For a start, Paul is talking about something kept secret, a truth previously hidden. Only at this stage of history – after the cross, after Pentecost – did God begin, principally through the Apostle Paul, to disclose the revelation that would define the period between the coming of the Spirit and the return of Christ to receive all believers to be with himself for ever, as he'd promised. In this third chapter of the Bible letter to Ephesus, Paul explains that Gentiles are now on an equal footing with Jews. When anyone believes in the Lord Jesus, and so receives Christ, he or she is born again spiritually and becomes a member of the Church that Christ calls 'his' or 'his body.'

Every Christian believer enters then into an eternal union with his or her saviour, who is the Head of the Church that's described metaphorically as his body (Ephesians 1:23). Christ and his Church will be eternal companions, so close that human marriage is the best way to picture it (Ephesians 5:22-33). This happens in the present Church Age. But after Christ returns to take his Bride, the Church, it's then God will begin another stage of his developing plan, with the focus once again returning to the Israelis:

"For then there will be a great tribulation, such as has not occurred since the beginning of the world until now, nor ever will. Unless those days had been cut short, no life would have been saved; but for the sake of the elect those days will be cut short" (Matthew 24:21-22).

It will be the toughest time ever to be on earth – certainly for Jewish believers who finally embrace Yehoshua as their messiah, but tough also for any who turn to the Lord then. In every stage or distinctive period of God's stewardship, God has his chosen ones. Whether it's the Old Testament period (Romans 11:2-5); the current Church Age (John 17:9; Ephesians 1:3); or that future time of Israel's trouble (Jeremiah 30:7; Matthew 24:22), we can read in our Bible about the elect of each of these distinct periods of God's dealings with our human race.

When that brief but troubled period is over, there will then be glorious and profound peace under the reign of Christ on this earth for a thousand years (Revelation 20:1-6). In the verses that follow, Paul describes this as another distinct time of God's stewardship known as the administration of the fullness of the times:

"In all wisdom and insight, He made known to us the mystery of His will, according to His kind intention which He purposed in Him with a view to an administration suitable to the fullness of the times, that is, the summing up of all things in Christ, things in the heavens and things on the earth" (Ephesians 1:8-10).

But even that's not the end, although it will be for this old world:

"the heavens will pass away with a roar and the elements will be destroyed with intense heat, and the earth and its works will be burned up. Since all these things are to be destroyed in this way, what sort of people ought you to be in holy conduct and godliness, looking for and hastening the coming of the day of God ... But according to His promise we are looking for new heavens and a new earth, in which righteousness dwells" (2 Peter 3:10-12).

That will finally be the end of history for this planet. The 'day of God' will have dawned as an eternal day. Till then, God is managing everything in its time to this glorious never ending.

13

FINAL WORD ON PRAYER

Let's begin by asking: 'What's the purpose of prayer? Is it to change God's mind? More basic than that, let's ask: 'Does prayer change God's mind?' The Bible says there are certain things the unchanging and unchangeable God has decreed from all eternity. Those things will inevitably come to pass.

No human being has ever had a more profound understanding of divine sovereignty than Jesus. No man ever prayed more effectively. In Gethsemane, he requested a different way. When that request was denied, he bowed to the Father's will. Here was perfect humanity modelling for us the perfect practice of prayer. In Matthew's record of Jesus' praying, we seem able to observe a change of some sort taking place. At first, he asks: "Let this cup pass from Me" (Matthew 26:39). Later, he emphasizes: 'Your will be done' (Matthew 26:42). The prayer of our Lord changed from "*If it is possible ...*" to "*If this cannot ...*" In other words, a change of wording in our Lord's request from "if it is possible" to "if it is not possible." All these changes occur between verses 39 and 42 of Matthew chapter 26.

Jesus, the perfect man, is giving us the perfect example of how we come to bow to the will of God through prayer. That prayer in Gethsemane was all about bowing to the perfect will of God; it was never about attempting to bend the perfect will of God. Both God's decree and Christ's prayer were already accounted for in the eternal counsels where the cross was planned by the triune God as the only possible means for any humans to be saved from eternal damnation on account of human rebellion.

We've been thinking about the question: 'Does prayer change God's mind?' The follow-up question is: 'If God knows everything already - including what he's going to do - does prayer actually work. Isn't it pointless?' We can straightaway rule out any idea of prayer being pointless. God both commands us to pray, and also invites us to make our requests known. James, writing in his letter near to the back of our Bibles, says we don't have because we don't ask (James 4:2). That implies we should ask, for the right things.

But much more than that, the promise of the Scriptures – proved by example - is that prayer does work. James again, who makes helpful contributions to our understanding of prayer, says: *"The prayer of a righteous person has great power as it is working"* (James 5:16). That does highlight a problem, however. The problem is we're not all that righteous. Someone has commented: "What prayer most often changes is the wickedness of our own hearts." I'm sure that's got to be correct, and, if so, that alone is reason enough to pray.

But let's come back again to the question: "If God knows everything, why pray?" The question assumes that prayer is one-dimensional – in other words, that it's all about supplication or intercession. On the contrary, prayer is multidimensional. It's a cliché perhaps, but the spectrum of prayer is more fully spelt out in the letters of the word 'acts' as A-C-T-S, where A stands for Adoration; C for Confession; T for Thanksgiving; and S for Supplication. The last part, supplication, is only one part or dimension of prayer.

God's sovereignty casts no shadow over the prayer of **adoration**. God's foreknowledge or determinate counsel doesn't negate the prayer of praise. The only thing it should do is give us greater reason for expressing our adoration for who God is! And in what way could God's sovereignty negatively affect the prayer of **confession**? I may not understand the relationship between divine sovereignty and human responsibility, but I do realize that what stems from the wickedness of my own heart doesn't line up with the will of God. We pray because we're guilty, pleading pardon from an offended God.

If anything, our understanding of God's sovereignty should provoke us to an intense prayer life of **thanksgiving**. We should see that every benefit, every good and perfect gift, is an expression of the abundance of his sovereign grace. We can thank God that all things work together or contribute in some way – under his sovereignty - for our long-term good of being made to be like Christ (Romans 8:28) and in that case we can give thanks in every circumstance (1 Thessalonians 5:18).

Now, we need to return to the case of the prayer of **supplication**. This is what we usually have in mind when we ask: 'Does prayer change things? And Bible examples would show us the answer is: 'Yes!' Before we share one of those Biblical examples, it may be worth reinforcing the distinction we've made there. Prayer doesn't change God's mind, because the God of the Bible is immutable, unchanging (Malachi 3:6). However, prayer changes things, because the God of the Bible is sovereign over all things. He himself doesn't change, but he changes things. Nothing outside of his own will can influence God, but he does influence everything. That is basic to the idea of the sovereignty of God that the Bible teaches.

Now, we'll come to the first of our biblical examples of prayer changing things. Take the case of Nineveh: When God hangs his sword of judgment over people's heads, and they repent; he then withholds his judgment. Ah, you say, that's my point - God changed his mind! No, I don't think that would be the correct conclusion to draw from that example (and others like it). The mind of God doesn't change, for God doesn't change. Things change - according to his sovereign will – and they change through secondary means and secondary activities in which prayer may be involved. The prayer of God's people is one of the means he uses to bring things to pass in this world (e.g. Daniel chapter 9).

The prayer that's effective is the prayer that's in keeping with God's will. The very reason we pray is because of God's sovereignty. God has it within his power to order (all) things according to his purpose. At this point, we should say something more about the will of God. When we talk loosely about the will of God, it's important to say what we mean exactly because there are differences in how the Bible speaks about God's will. We talked earlier of how Jesus prayed in the Garden of Gethsemane, confirming it was his father's will that he should die on the cross. It was. There could be no alternative. Before the world began to exist, it had been decreed that the Son of God, as man, would die to pay for human disobedience.

This was something that was predetermined (Acts 2:23). How right it was for Jesus to pray in the terms in which he did. How sure we can be also from God's Word that there could never be any change in the decree. Not in that decree nor in any other matter which God has similarly appointed (for example, the stumbling of Israel as a nation); indeed, no change is possible in anything that's subject to God's foreordination or sovereign predestining grace (in particular, an individual's salvation). Some people refer to this as God's 'decretive' (or predestined) will.

Let's now shift the focus somewhat. Before Jesus returned to heaven, he commanded his Apostles to make other disciples, to baptize them, and to teach them to observe all the things he'd commanded them. Our Lord, who is the one with total authority in heaven and on earth, didn't leave his followers to make up their own minds about how to follow him. Christianity is principally a relationship with Christ, that's true; but there are rules or precepts laid down in the Bible for us to obey. We don't need to enquire from God if baptism is the right step for us to take after receiving Christ, any more than we need to pray to confirm it's wrong to sleep with someone who isn't our spouse. There's only one thing to be done with the Lord's precepts, and that's to obey them. Some people refer to these commands as the 'preceptive' (or prescriptive) will of God – because obviously his will is spelt out there in the precepts contained in our Bible. Again, there's no wiggle room.

Then we come to what God wants. This is very different from what God decrees. His decrees always come to pass. But God doesn't always get what he wants. For example, we read: *"[God] who desires all people to be saved and to come to the knowledge of the truth"* (1 Timothy 2:4). Some Bible versions translate this as *"God wills all to be saved"* rather than God desires it. But to use the word 'will' here allows possible confusion with God's will by decree. That cannot be in view here or we would end up with the teaching of universalism. Universalism - which teaches all people will end up saved from eternal judgement - is plainly wrong, as Christ spoke of those who suffer the fire of eternal punishment (Matthew 25:41,46).

God's expressed desire here won't be fully realized, but this statement does emphasize that God takes no pleasure in the death and judgement of the wicked. It's perfectly correct for us to express to God a desire for someone's salvation (see Romans 10:1), while still being convinced by scripture that it's those who are appointed to eternal life who will believe (Acts 13:48). We pray, not knowing who are appointed to life; Christ who did know, prayed for those whom the father had given to him (John 17:9). John's Gospel, especially in chapters 6 and 17, makes it clear that Christ's death was effective for all for whom God intended it to be.

In summary then, prayer cannot change God's mind because *predestined & prescribed* things are unalterable; prayer can change things because *preferred* timings of judgements may be *permitted* some change (Jeremiah 18:6-10; Amos 7:3; 7:6; 8:2); but prayer does change us – because by it *personal* character is shaped and duties directed. It's good to allow ourselves to be influenced through the practice of God's presence until our desires reflect his desires (Psalm 37:4). In other words, most importantly, prayer changes us.

God only permits those things which will lead to the accomplishment of his decrees (Genesis 50:20). There are times when God wants us at a certain place, doing a certain thing (Acts 16:6-10), and so it's good to pray about it. But God's personal guidance in our lives never violates either his decrees or his precepts.

14

THE OPENING OF THE SCROLL

Cicero once apologized for Jupiter's neglect of earthly affairs. He stated that the sovereign of the universe was on the whole a good sovereign, but with so much business on his hands, he had no time to look into details. The God of the Bible is shown to be totally otherwise. Never for one moment does he let go of the reins of the universe. No detail escapes his attention, but everything is exposed to his view (Hebrews 4:13). When some asked: 'Where was God on the 11th September 2001, the answer had to be: 'The same as where he was on the 10th and 12th of September.'

As we approach a conclusion of a series of studies on God's sovereignty, what could be more fitting than to glimpse with the Apostle John the insight into the eternal future he was privileged to have revealed to him? Before that, he saw the sovereign God upon his throne. As through an open door, he was permitted to see into the throne room of heaven. What he saw there is described to us in Revelation chapter 4.

It's been said that Revelation chapter 4 is to Revelation chapter 5 what a scene-setting is to a drama. God's transcendent glory is first described in chapter 4. Then the drama unfolds in chapter 5, because in the right hand of *"him who sits on the throne"* – as God is so often referred to in the book – we're told there's a scroll, close sealed with seven seals.

Our attention zooms in on this scroll. But what's in it? What does it contain? From the context of all that follows, it would seem likely that this scroll contains all of God's purposes for the judgment of the entire universe – whether for damnation or for glorification. In the symbolism of the day in which John lived, whatever is in that scroll can be enacted only if you break the seal. And so, in the heavenly drama too, this scroll with all of God's purposes is sealed with 7 seals and a mighty angel challenges the entire universe: Who is worthy to approach this God and take the scroll from his right hand? Who is worthy to break the seals, and so enact, to bring about all of God's purposes of vindication or the otherwise appropriate recompense? And no one is found who is worthy. Neither cherubim nor seraphim, not the elders, no one on the earth, no one under the earth in the abodes of the dead. And John weeps, not because his curiosity had got the better of him. But, because in the symbolism of the vision, this means that God's purposes for judgement, justice and blessing will not be brought to pass. It means justice won't be served upon all that's transpired on earth throughout history.

We long for moral justice, do we not? Every day, the newspapers and media spotlight the plight of someone who didn't get what they deserve. The widow of a murdered police officer demands a retrial if the worst the perpetrators are accused of is the reduced charge of manslaughter. Suspected felons walk free from court because of some technicality with the prosecution case or the evidence. And I suspect that even those whom society as a whole has judged guilty of terrible war crimes might fancy their chances if allowed to explain their ideology and were permitted to advance mitigating factors. It's one of the four cornerstones of any adequate worldview: that it must account for morality, which includes the desire for, and basis of, moral justice. At the end of God's Book, this scene, unfolding from Revelation chapter 5, reassures all victims and villains who have ever lived that an ultimate judgement day is coming.

However, the Apostle John will get to see what the scroll contains. As is stated in other places in the Bible, God the Father, the ancient of days, has entrusted all judgement into the hands of the Son of Man, the God-man, Jesus of Nazareth. He's introduced here to John as the Lion of the tribe of Judah, but John turns and sees a Lamb. This is the most glorious and sublime mixed metaphor that could ever be. The Lion who is the Lamb comes from the throne itself and takes the scroll out of the hand of him who sits on the throne. He alone is found worthy to bring about all of God's purposes for judgement and blessing. As the Apostle Paul announced to the Athenians, it is the man whom God raised from the dead after his crucifixion at Jerusalem who will be the judge of all.

As John watches in the vision, he sees the seals of the scroll being opened in turn, and he witnesses how, graphically depicted in apocalyptic visions rich in symbolism, God's judgments begin to fall upon those living on the earth towards the end of time. As the reader watches with John, he or she hears heaven's verdict: that all God's ways are righteous and true (e.g. Revelation 19:2). Then we come to the never-ending end to the last Book of the Bible.

In contrast with the chilling way in which never-ending punishment is described for all who have rejected God's way of salvation, which salvation was ultimately shown to be through Christ, John describes for us a scene that seems almost to defy description – and that is the glory of the environment that all who have trusted in the Lord will enjoy for ever, world without end. We'll confine ourselves to asking: what is shown to be new; what is shown to be missing; what is shown to be central?

First then, what's new? There's a new heaven and earth in which righteousness dwells (2 Peter 3:13). And located on the new earth is the new Jerusalem. Its main features are fleshed out with four images:

- First, it's a city: the perfect version of what once stood for complete fellowship in the place of God's choice in historic Jerusalem.
- Second, it's a cube: for the innermost part of both Moses' Tabernacle and Solomon's Temple was a cube where God's most intimate presence was specially known, but to which at those early times access was most restricted.
- Third, it's a bride: and perhaps this imagery captures the thrill of the most intimate relationship, where the honeymoon never ends.
- Fourth, it's a tabernacle: where God's desire to reside on earth among humans is ultimately satisfied (Zephaniah 3:17).

And what's missing, I'm sure we want to know? Well, Life will never hurt again, nor will bad things happen. Tears, pain, sadness, death, the curse will all be consigned to history, never more to return. Also, there's no Temple; life will no longer be split between the religious and the secular. And no sun and moon, with the possible meaning that there'll be no more danger and so no more protection necessary. That is, if we can be guided by the psalmist here: *"The sun will not smite you by day, Nor the moon by night"* (Psalm 121:6). There will also be no sea anymore. That is, the new world will be without any restless sea which surfaces things best left buried – as Isaiah graphically described it: *"But the wicked are like the tossing sea, For it cannot be quiet, And its waters toss up refuse and mud. 'There is no peace,' says my God, 'for the wicked'"* (Isaiah 57:20-21). More wonderfully, there will be no impurity. Nothing to spoil the pure enjoyment of unsullied relationships.

And so finally, we should ask: 'What's central? Well, there's the fountain of living waters. Surely that has to symbolize God's unending, abundant supply, as the psalmist said: *"How precious is Your lovingkindness, O God! And the children of men take refuge in the shadow of Your wings. They drink their fill of the abundance of Your house; And You give them to drink of the river of Your delights. For with You is the fountain of life; In Your light we see light"* (Psalm 36:7-9).

Most precious of all, central to this whole scene are the throne of God, the Lamb, and God himself. What a thought! God – and not self - will be at the centre of our existence for ever and ever! For sin with its self-centredness will never more invade our thoughts and behaviours. Oh, that we could live our future life now (as helped by his Spirit we can, in part)!

Now we see God's master-plan of the ages: it's to have everything united under and gathered around Christ (cp. The foretaste in the 'summing up' of Ephesians 1:10). To fully get the picture here, think of how a preacher draws his message to a conclusion. He recapitulates his main point as the summation of all he's said. Just like that, God will bring everything (that's in view here) into a state of being 'summed up' in Christ – which has always been God's sovereign master-plan – that Christ should be central. This is our destiny. Amen!

15

EPILOGUE

In this book we've majored on God's sovereignty (as the one 'who works all things after the counsel of His will,' Ephesians 1:11) with only some hints as to what that means for human freedom. Having completed our focus on God, it may not be out of place to attempt to deal briefly with the related and often problematic topic of human freewill. As we'll review, 'freedom' is a confusing term!

Suppose someone says: 'Since you maintain that God is sovereign, then it must be that humans are not free.' Well, as you might guess, it all depends on what you mean by 'free.' We are free from coercion, but we are not free from our fallen nature. It's not necessary – or even correct – to think of human freedom beginning where God's sovereignty ends. Let's expand on that ...

Biblical thinkers in dealing with humanity have tended to distinguish between freedom and freewill. Even in a Pre-Fall world, human freedom was not absolute liberty for that can only be true of God. God is the only being who is not influenced by anything outside of himself. In contrast, God's dependent creatures can only, in the very nature of things, have limited freedom even if real.

If God knows that something is going to happen, it's certain to happen. It cannot not happen. But that doesn't mean God forces it to happen. God works out his sovereignty - his supreme freedom - in, by, and through the real choices of his creatures in such a way that his creatures are not forced to act. This is the conclusion we may draw from the Apostle Paul when he dismisses the objection: *"Why does He still find fault? For who resists His will?"* (Romans 9:19). Paul terminates his argument on that note: as if he says it's a mystery – but not a contradiction - how God works out his supreme will using the real choices of his creatures.

Let's mention the unpopular idea of 'determinism,' since that idea often surfaces when God's sovereignty is being stressed. Determinism is external coercion. Freedom, by contrast, is self-determination. We must live under one system or the other: either freedom or determinism, and biblically we believe it to be freedom. It's a freedom that's limited but real. Adam's sin was, or at least involved, the quest for autonomy, the desire to increase his real freedom to absolute freedom like that of the creator. As a result, our freedom is now additionally without the moral ability to choose for good or for God.

Adam before the Fall had both the ability to sin and the ability to not sin. After the Fall, the moral condition of original sin that applies to us all is tragically the inability to not sin. That's not to say we've lost freewill, however. After the Fall, we still have a will that is free in the sense that it is not coerced by any external agency or power. We still have the ability to make choices according to our own desires; now, however, the human will is in a state of corruption. We are still free to do what we want, but the problem lies in what we want. We lost any innate desire to seek and to please God. We lack the freedom to do or choose good as well as evil.

Our freedom was never absolute, but additionally, we're now in bondage to our corrupted nature.

The big issue is how a person can regain liberty - the moral ability to choose what is good, to choose the things of God. Since fallen man is spiritually dead, he is a slave to himself, to his passions and lusts; he follows the desires of his evil heart. This is the Lord's teaching in John 8 when he taught the disbelieving Jews that the truth would make them free (v.32). Like so many today, they did not see themselves as anything other than free or as anything other than basically good. The Lord told them *"everyone who commits sin is the slave of sin"* (v.34). The liberation of fallen humanity absolutely requires God's grace – *"if the Son makes you free, you will be free indeed"* (v.36).

It seems fitting to sign off with a text that offers us a glimpse of God's sovereign holiness, as well as the corrupted state of human nature, and symbolically God's gracious remedy through the cross of Christ.

"In the year of King Uzziah's death I saw the Lord sitting on a throne, lofty and exalted, with the train of His robe filling the temple. Seraphim stood above Him, each having six wings: with two he covered his face, and with two he covered his feet, and with two he flew. And one called out to another and said, "Holy, Holy, Holy, is the LORD of hosts, The whole earth is full of His glory." And the foundations of the thresholds trembled at the voice of him who called out, while the temple was filling with smoke.

Then I said, "Woe is me, for I am ruined! Because I am a man of unclean lips, And I live among a people of unclean lips; For my eyes have seen the King, the LORD of hosts." Then one of the seraphim flew to me with a burning coal in his hand, which he had taken from the altar with tongs. He touched my mouth with it and said, "Behold, this has touched your lips; and your iniquity

EPILOGUE

is taken away and your sin is forgiven." (Isaiah 6:1-7).

MORE BOOKS BY THE AUTHOR

- 60 Minutes to Raise the Dead
- 8 Amazing Privileges of God's People: A Bible Study of Romans 9:4-5
- A Christ-Centred Faith
- A Crisis of Identity : Who God Wants Us To Be As Christians
- A Tale of Two Women: Life Lessons from the Book of Proverbs
- A Test of Commitment: 15 Challenges to Stimulate Your Devotion to Christ
- About the Bush: The Five Excuses of Moses
- Abraham: Friend of God
- After God's Own Heart - The Life of David
- Amazing Grace! Paul's Gospel Message to the Galatians
- An Unchanging God? Exploring the Allegation of Divine Inconsistency
- AWOL! Bible Deserters & Defectors
- Bible Answers For Big Questions
- Bible Answers to Listeners' Questions
- Certainty in the Face of Change! The Epistles of John
- Christ-centred Faith
- Christian Friendship: Closer Than A Brother?
- Christianity 101 - 7 Bible Basics
- Daniel Decoded: Deciphering Bible Prophecy
- Deepening Our Relationship With Christ
- Does Anyone Know Why We're Here?: Answers from Ecclesiastes

MORE BOOKS BY THE AUTHOR

- Double Vision: Hidden Meanings in the Prophecy of Isaiah
- Edge of Eternity: Approaching the End of Life
- Encounters At The Cross
- Esther: A Date With Destiny
- Experiencing God in Ephesians
- Exploring Issues of Life – A Challenge to Live as God Intended
- Fencepost Turtles: People Placed by God
- First Corinthians: Nothing But Christ Crucified
- Five Sacred Solos: The Truths That the Reformation Recovered
- Five Women And A Baby: The Genealogy of Jesus
- Get Real! Living Everyday as An Authentic Follower of Christ
- Going the Distance: How to Avoid A Spiritual Knock-Out
- Great Spiritual Movements
- Great Truths of the Gospel .... And the Errors People Often Make About It
- Healthy Churches – God's Bible Blueprint For Growth
- Home Truths – Life Lessons from the "Home' Life of Joseph and the Parental Care of Paul for the Thessalonians
- Hope for Humanity – God's Fix for a Broken World
- If Atheism is True... The Futile Faith and Hopeless Hypotheses of Dawkins & Co.
- Increasing Your Christian Footprint: A Dig into the Old Testament Gilgals
- Jesus – What Does The Bible Really Say?
- Jesus: Son Over God's House
- Knowing God: Reflections on Psalm 23
- Learning from Bible Grandparents
- Learning How To Pray – From the Lord's Prayer
- Legacy of Kings: Israel's Chequered History
- Life...the Universe...and Ultimate Answers
- Living in God's House: His Design in Action

- Mindfulness That Jesus Endorses
- Minor Prophets: Major Issues
- No Compromise!
- Once Saved, Always Saved? The Reality of Eternal Security
- Our Adoption as Sons
- Overcoming Objections to Christian Faith
- Power Outage: Christianity Unplugged
- Praying With Paul
- Pure Christianity - The Essence of Biblical Discipleship
- Pure Milk: Nurturing New Life in Jesus
- Really Good News for Today!
- Salt and the Sacrifice of Christ
- Samson: A Type of Christ
- Seeds - A Potted Bible History
- Sowing in Hard Soil: Tools and Encouragement for Preaching the Gospel
- Stronger than the Storm - The Last Words of Jesus
- Take Your Mark's Gospel
- The Book of James - Epistle of Straw?
- The Character of Christ in Paul's Letters
- The Feasts of Jehovah in One Hour
- The Future in Bible Prophecy
- The Glory of God - What It Is and Why It Matters
- The Kingdom of God - Past, Present or Future
- The Supremacy of Christ - A Bible Study of Jesus
- The Tabernacle - God's House of Shadows
- The Visions of Zechariah
- Total Conviction - 4 Things God Wants You to Be Really Convinced About
- Trees of the Bible
- Tribes and Tribulations: Israel's Predicted Personalities

MORE BOOKS BY THE AUTHOR

- Turning the World Upside Down: Seven Revolutionary Christian Ideas
- Unlocking Hebrews
- Windows to Faith

ABOUT THE AUTHOR

Born and educated in Scotland, Brian worked as a government scientist until God called him into full-time Christian ministry on behalf of the Churches of God (www.churchesofgod.info). His voice has been heard on Search For Truth radio broadcasts for over 30 years (visit www.searchfortruth.podbean.com) during which time he has been an itinerant Bible teacher throughout the UK. His evangelical and missionary work outside the UK is primarily in Belgium, The Philippines and South East Central Africa. He is married to Rosemary, with a son and daughter.

ABOUT THE PUBLISHER

Hayes Press (www.hayespress.org) is a registered charity in the United Kingdom, whose primary mission is to disseminate the Word of God, mainly through literature. It is one of the largest distributors of gospel tracts and leaflets in the United Kingdom, with over 100 titles and many thousands dispatched annually. In addition to paperbacks and eBooks, Hayes Press also publishes Plus Eagles' Wings, a fun and educational Bible magazine for children, and Golden Bells, a popular daily Bible reading calendar in wall or desk formats.

If you would like to contact Hayes Press, there are a number of ways you can do so:

By mail: c/o The Barn, Flaxlands, Royal Wootton Bassett, Wiltshire, UK SN4 8DY

By phone: 01793 850598

By eMail: info@hayespress.org

via Facebook: www.facebook.com/hayespress.org

www.ingramcontent.com/pod-product-compliance
Lightning Source LLC
Chambersburg PA
CBHW071307040426
42444CB00009B/1912